CHILDCRAFT

THE HOW AND WHY LIBRARY

ABOUT YOU

World Book, Inc.
a Scott Fetzer company
Chicago

Childcraft—The How and Why Library

World Book, Inc.
233 N. Michigan Avenue
Chicago, IL 60601

The Library of Congress has cataloged a previous edition of this title as follows.

Childcraft: the how and why library.
v. cm.
Summary: Presents illustrated articles, stories, and poems, grouped thematically in fifteen volumes.
Includes bibliographical references and indexes.
Contents: v. 1. Poems and rhymes -- v. 2. Once upon a time -- v. 3. Art around us -- v. 4. The world of animals -- v. 5 The world of plants -- v. 6. Our earth -- v. 7. The universe -- v. 8. How does it happen? -- v. 9. How things work -- v. 10. Shapes and numbers -- v. 11. About you -- v. 12. Who we are -- v. 13. See the world -- v. 14. Celebrate! -- v. 15. Guide and index.
ISBN 0-7166-2203-3 (set)
1. Children's encyclopedias and dictionaries. [1. Encyclopedias and dictionaries.] I. Title: Childcraft. II. World Book, Inc.
AG6 .C48 2004
031--dc21 2003008722

This edition:

ISBN-13: 978-0-7166-2219-2 (set)
ISBN-10: 0-7166-2219-X (set)
ISBN-13: 978-0-7166-2230-7 (Volume 11, About You)
ISBN-10: 0-7166-2230-0 (Volume 11, About You)

Printed in China
4 5 6 7 8 9 09 08 07 06

For information on other World Book publications, visit our Web site at **http://www.worldbook.com** or call **1-800 WORLDBK (967-5325)**. For information on sales to schools and libraries, call **1-800-975-3250 (United States),** or **1-800-837-5365 (Canada).**

Contents

Introduction

This book is about you. It is about what goes on outside and inside your body. It is about why you have hair and skin, toenails and fingernails. It's about your bones, muscles, blood, heart, stomach, and brain. It's about your senses of sight, hearing, smell, taste, and touch. It's about how you were born, how you've grown, how you are still growing, and what you will be like when you are grown up. It's also about what goes on in your mind—your thoughts and feelings. Finally, it's about taking care of yourself so that you can continue to grow strong and healthy.

You may wonder how there can be a book about you, when you didn't help write it, and there are no pictures of you in it. It's because even though there is no one in the world exactly like you, all people have many things in common. All people have a human body. All people are born. All people have feelings. All people eat.

There are many features in this book to help you find your way through it. You will find fun-filled facts in the boxes marked **Know It All!** You can amaze your friends with what you know!

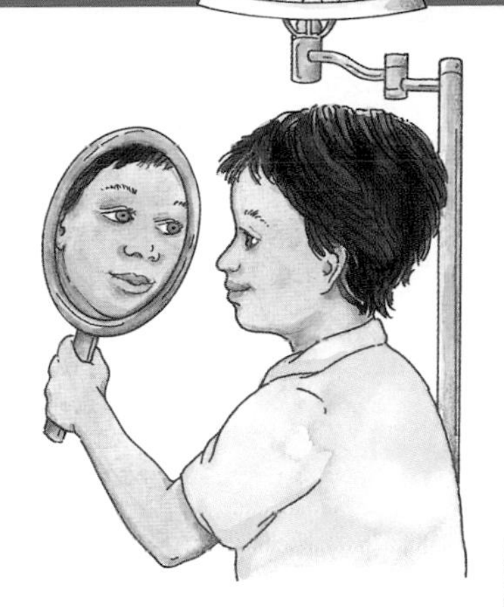

This book also has many activities that you can do at home. Look for the words **Try This!** over a colored ball. The activity that follows offers a way to learn about your body. For example, you can check your pulse to find out how fast your heart is beating, play a game to test your senses of taste and smell, or make puppets to show your feelings.

Each activity has a number in its colored ball. Activities with a 1 in a green ball are simplest to do. Those with a 2 in a yellow ball may require a little adult help with tasks such as cutting, measuring, or using hot water. Activities with a 3 in a red ball may need more adult help.

A Try This! activity that has a colorful border around its entire page is a little

KNOW It All!

Know It All! boxes have fun-filled facts.

Each activity has a number. The higher the number, the more adult help you may need.

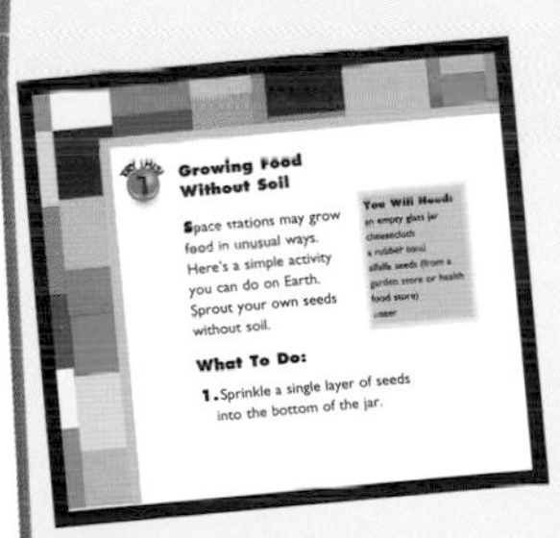

Growing Food Without Soil

Space stations may grow food in unusual ways. Here's a simple activity you can do on Earth. Sprout your own seeds without soil.

You Will Need:
an empty glass jar
cheesecloth
a rubber band
alfalfa seeds (from a garden store or health food store)
water

What To Do:

1. Sprinkle a single layer of seeds into the bottom of the jar.

An activity that has this colorful border is a little more complex than one without the border.

more complex or requires a few more materials. Take a moment to review the list of materials and to read through the instructions before you begin.

As you read this book, you will see that some words are printed in bold type, **like this.** These are words that might be new to you. You can find the meanings and pronunciations of these words in the **Glossary** at the back of the book. Turn to the **Index** to look up page numbers of subjects that interest you the most.

If you enjoy learning about your body, find out more about it in other resources, such as those listed below. Check them out at a bookstore or at your library.

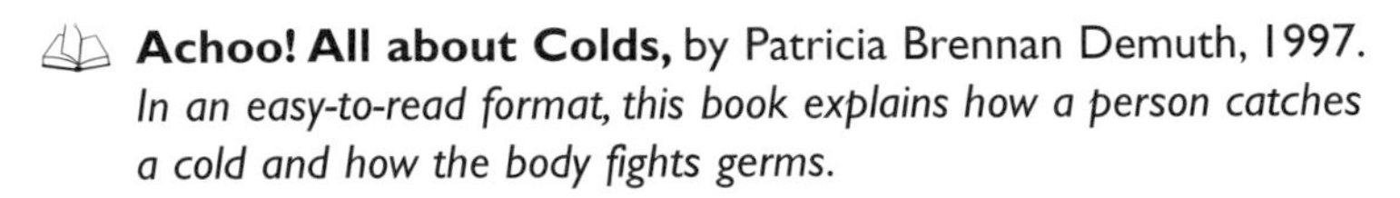

- **Achoo! All about Colds,** by Patricia Brennan Demuth, 1997. *In an easy-to-read format, this book explains how a person catches a cold and how the body fights germs.*
- **The Amazing Pull-out Pop-up Body in a Book,** by David Hawcock, 1997. *Open this book to unfold an illustrated 5-foot tall, 3-D skeleton complete with bones, muscles, and organs.*
- **Dr. Kanner, Dentist with a Smile,** by Alice Flanagan, 1997. *A child is introduced to a dentist and his work. The tools the dentist uses in caring for teeth are also explained.*
- **How to Be a Friend: A Guide to Making Friends and Keeping Them,** by Laurie Krasny Brown and Marc Brown, 2001. *Dinosaur characters show the value of friends and how to make friends. From the creators of the "Dino Life Guides for Families" series.*
- **I Did It, I'm Sorry,** by Mark and Caralyn Buehner, 1998. *This is a wacky quiz book that points the way to good behavior.*
- **The Magic School Bus Explores the Senses,** by Joanna Cole and Bruce Degen, 2001. *In this latest adventure, Ms. Frizzle's class learns about sight, smell, hearing, taste, and touch.*
- **Ultimate Human Body 2.0,** CD-ROM for Mac and Windows DK Multimedia Software, 1997. *On this CD you can rotate virtual body organs and use the 3-D scanner to zoom in and out of the various systems of the body.*
- **Where Do Babies Come From?,** by Angela Royston, 2001. *A simple introduction to the concept of reproduction, starting with animals and plants and then turning to the human baby.*
- **Why Do My Feet Fall Asleep and Other Questions About the Circulatory System,** by Sharon Cromwell, 1998. *Check out the other titles in this "Body Wise" series as well to learn all about the systems of the body.*

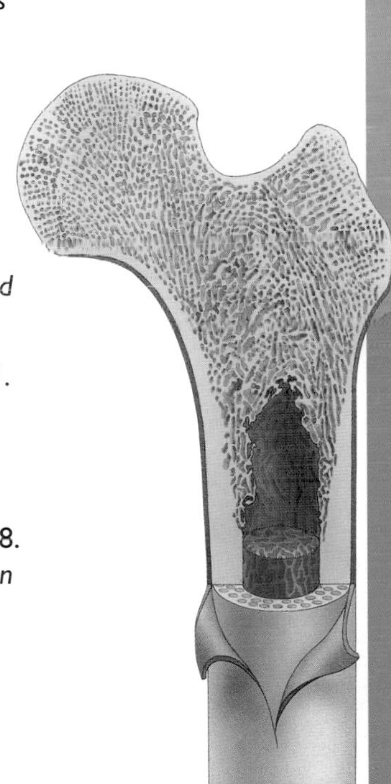

Outside of You

Millions of people live in the world. Not one of them looks exactly like you. Your look is truly special.

No one else has precisely your nose or exactly your skin color. No one else has a smile just like yours, or the exact same fingerprints. You may look a little—or even a lot—like someone else, especially someone in your family. But there is no one, not even if you have a twin, that looks like you do in every way. You are really one of a kind.

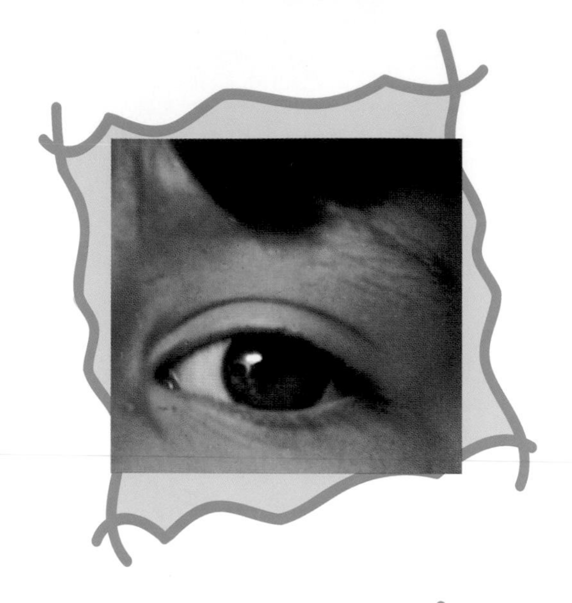

Face to Face

Look at your face in a mirror.

What do you see?

You see two eyes, a nose, and a mouth.

What else do you see?

You see eyebrows, and you see eyelashes. These tiny hairs keep dirt and dust out of your eyes.

Look deep into your eyes. The colored circle is your iris. What color is your iris?

Look closely at your nose. Your nose has two holes in it called nostrils (NAH struhlz). The air you breathe and the scents you smell go in through your nostrils.

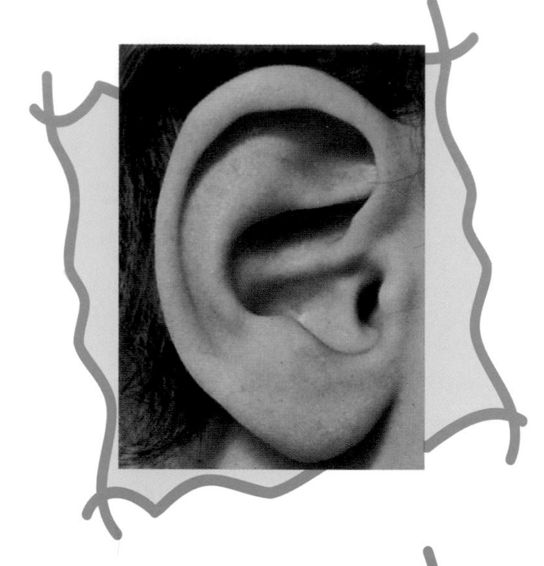

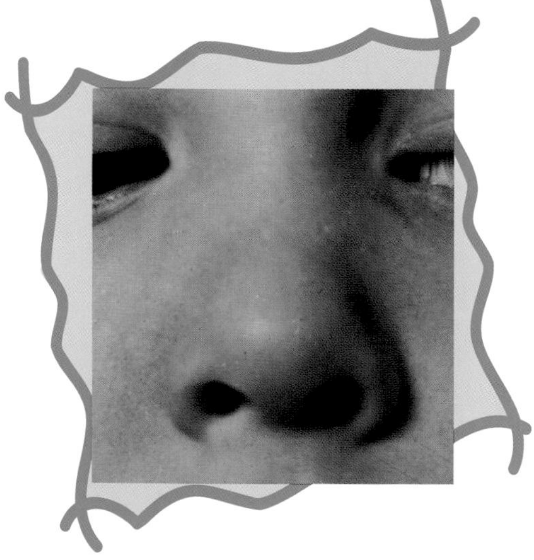

Take a close look at your face. You will find that yours is like no one else's.

Below your nose is your mouth. You use your mouth for eating, drinking, breathing, and talking.

On the sides of your head are your ears. The parts of your ears you can see catch sounds and send them inside your ears.

In many ways, your face is like everyone else's face. Everyone has a mouth, nose, eyes, and ears. But yours have shapes and sizes all their own.

Put them together, and they make your own **unique** (yoo NEEK) face.

One You, Two Sides

Your head has two sides, a right side and a left side. Each side has an eye, a cheek, an eyebrow, an ear, and a nostril. So, do both sides look the same? Take a closer look and see.

Look at yourself in a mirror.

Are your eyebrows exactly alike? Or is one more curved than the other?

Are your ears in exactly the same place on each side of your head? Do they have the same shape?

Does your nose have the same shape on both sides?

What about your hair? Does it look the same on both sides?

Do your eyes have the same shape?

This half was copied.

In these pictures, one side of the girl's face has been exactly copied to make the other side. Does the girl look the same in both pictures?

This half was copied.

Now you can probably see that each side of your face is a bit different. This is okay. Everyone has two different sides.

Other parts of your body do not match exactly, either. Look at your hands. Is one bigger than the other? How about your feet? Do the toes on each foot have different shapes?

TRY THIS! 1

What if the two sides of your face were exactly alike? What would you look like? Try this and see. Find a photo of yourself. Hold a mirror along the nose as shown here. Does the new "picture" of you look like you? Turn the mirror around and look at the other half. Does this "picture" look the same as the first one?

Let's Talk Teeth!

When you were a newborn baby, no one could see your teeth. They were just little tooth buds hidden in your gums. There they waited to grow. When you were between 6 months and 1 year old, your baby teeth began to break through your gums. By the time you were about 2 years old, you had all 20 of your baby teeth.

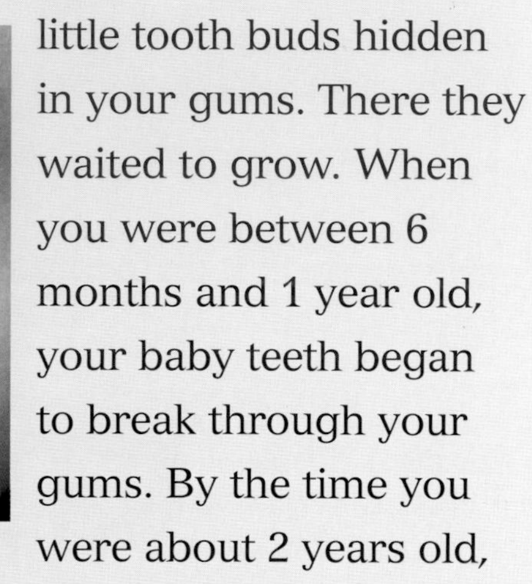

Your permanent (PUR muh nuhnt) teeth start to come in when you are about 6 years old. If you do not have them yet, you soon will. One by one they will push out your baby teeth.

When all your permanent teeth come in, you will have 32 teeth. That may seem like

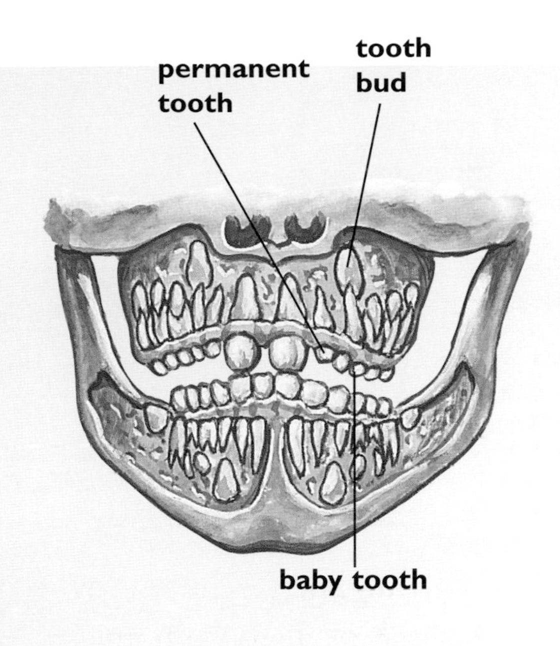

a lot of teeth for your mouth, but your jaw will grow to make room for them.

Your teeth all together make a great smile. Each tooth also has a special job. The teeth at the front of your mouth are shaped to cut food. The pointed teeth next to them are made to grip and tear food. At the back of your mouth are flat teeth for chewing. All your teeth work together to break food into little pieces that are easier for you to swallow.

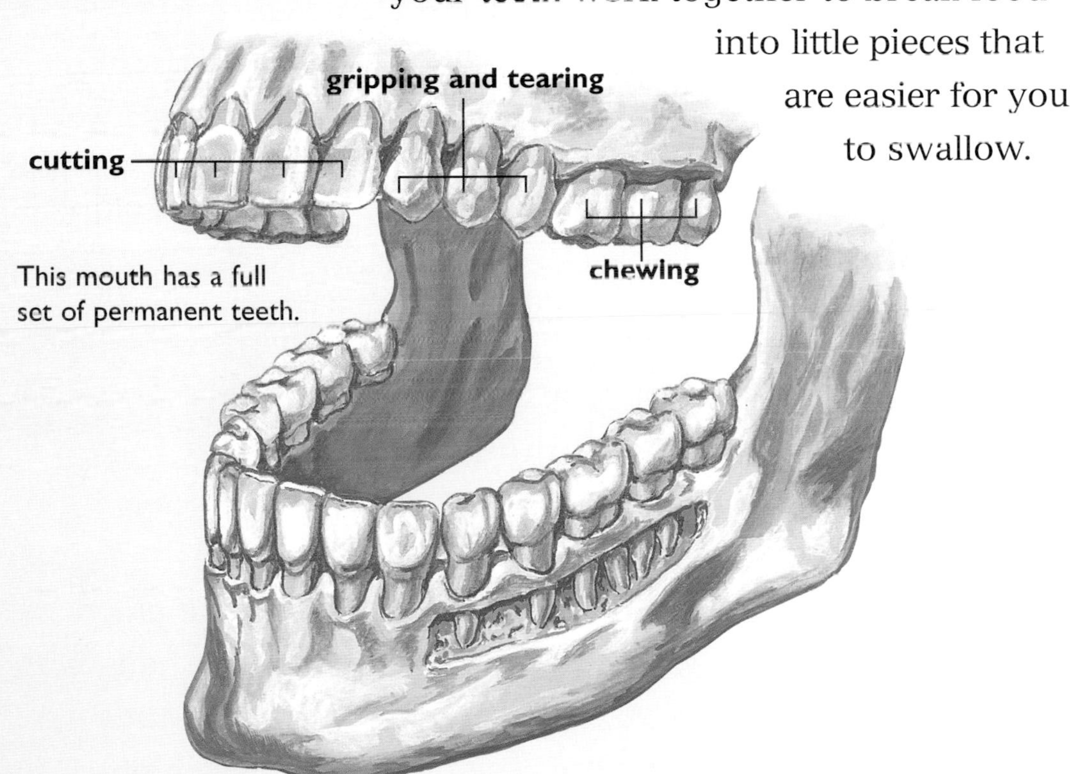

This mouth has a full set of permanent teeth.

Here's to Hair

Your body is covered with hair. Tiny hairs grow over most of your body. Thick hairs grow from your head. The only places on your body where hair does not grow are the palms of your hands and the soles of your feet.

Each hair grows out of a tiny sac (sak), "a little pocket" in your skin. The sac is called a **follicle** (FAH luh kuhl). At the bottom of each follicle is a supply of blood for the hair. The blood makes the hair grow. Around each hair there is a little supply of oil. The oil makes hair shine.

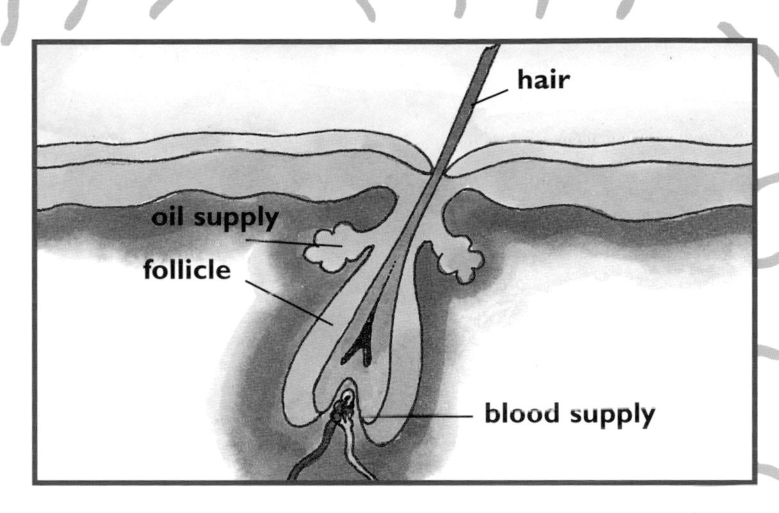

And each tiny sac has a muscle that makes your hair stand on end when you are cold or scared.

Have you ever wondered why some hairs grow long while others never do? This happens because hairs grow for only a certain amount of time. Then the follicles take a rest. When a new hair starts to grow, the old hair falls out. The hair on your head grows for a long time. Other hairs grow for only a short time.

A straight hair is round. A curly hair is also round, but it has little flat places on it. The more flat places there are, the curlier the hair.

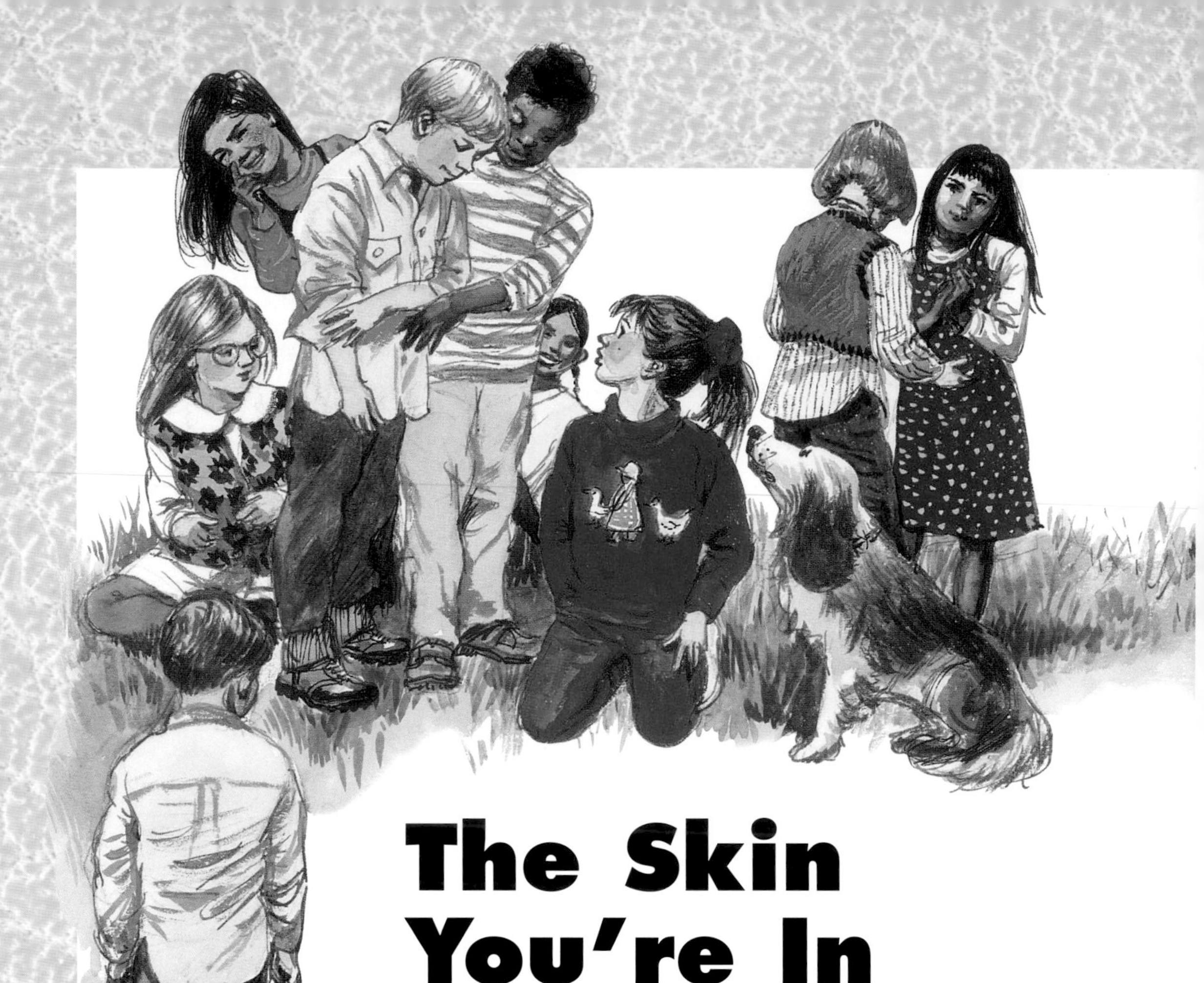

The Skin You're In

Everybody is covered with skin.

Look all over your body. What do you see everywhere you look? The answer is skin! Skin covers your entire body, and it protects your body in many ways.

Your body needs certain fluids (FLOO ihdz), such as water and blood, to work. Your skin keeps these fluids in. Your skin keeps out things that can make you sick. It also helps keep your body at a certain temperature.

KNOW It All!

The skin on the soles of your feet is the toughest skin on your body. It is also the thickest. The thinnest skin is on your eyelids.

All skin is made up of three layers. The outer layer is about as thin as a piece of paper. This is where most of your skin's growth takes place. The middle layer is much thicker than the first layer. It contains blood and hair follicles. This is also where sweat is made. Under this layer is another layer. It contains fat and blood vessels.

Your skin has tiny holes called **pores** (pohrz). When you are hot, sweat comes out through your pores. As the sweat dries, you feel cooler. When you are cold, your pores close and no sweat gets out.

Sometimes when you are cold, you shiver. Shivering helps to warm you. It is caused by muscles moving in your skin.

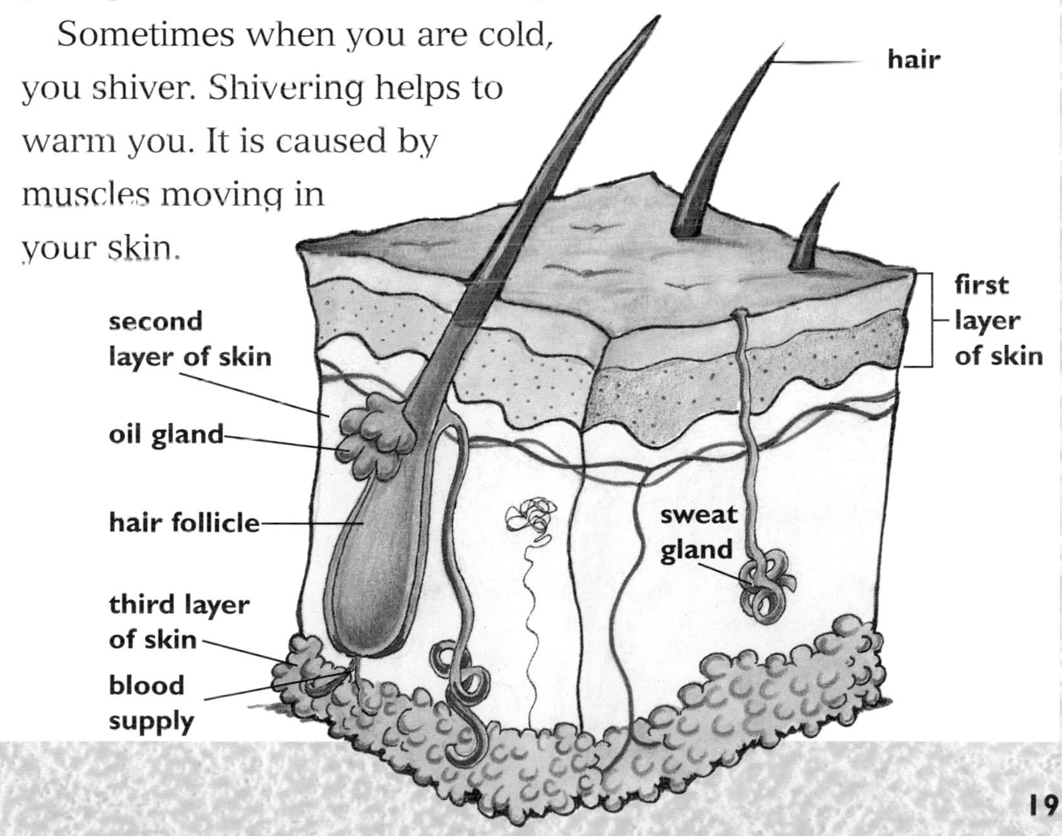

Why Is Skin Different Colors?

Around the world—and in your own neighborhood—people's skin colors are different. Some have light brown skin, some have dark skin, some have yellow skin, and some have skin that is pink, almost white.

Most of the color of your skin comes from a chemical called **melanin** (MEHL uh nihn). Melanin is made inside your skin, hair, and eyes.

Everyone, no matter what color their skin is, has some melanin. But different people's bodies make different amounts of melanin. The less melanin they make, the lighter their skin.

People with light colored skin have less melanin.

KNOW It All!

Sometimes, melanin builds up in small spots. These spots are called freckles. People who have freckles may get even more of these spots if they spend a lot of time in the sun.

People who come from hot countries make more melanin. This helps protect them from the sun's burning rays. Melanin protects the body by absorbing, or taking in, the sun's burning rays.

The amount of melanin your body makes, and therefore your skin color, comes from your parents. But skin makes more melanin when sunlight hits it. This extra melanin tans skin.

People with darker skin have more melanin.

What Hands and Feet Can Do

Your hands and feet help you do all kinds of things.

Each hand has four fingers and a thumb. Your fingers and thumbs pick up things and hold them.

Kicking a ball is just one thing you can do with your feet.

Your fingers and thumbs are good tools. You use them to button your shirt, tie your shoelaces, turn the pages of a book, and move the mouse on a computer.

Your fingers touch and feel things too. They help you know whether something is hot or cold, soft or hard, smooth, rough, or prickly.

You also use your hands to protect yourself. They shield your eyes from

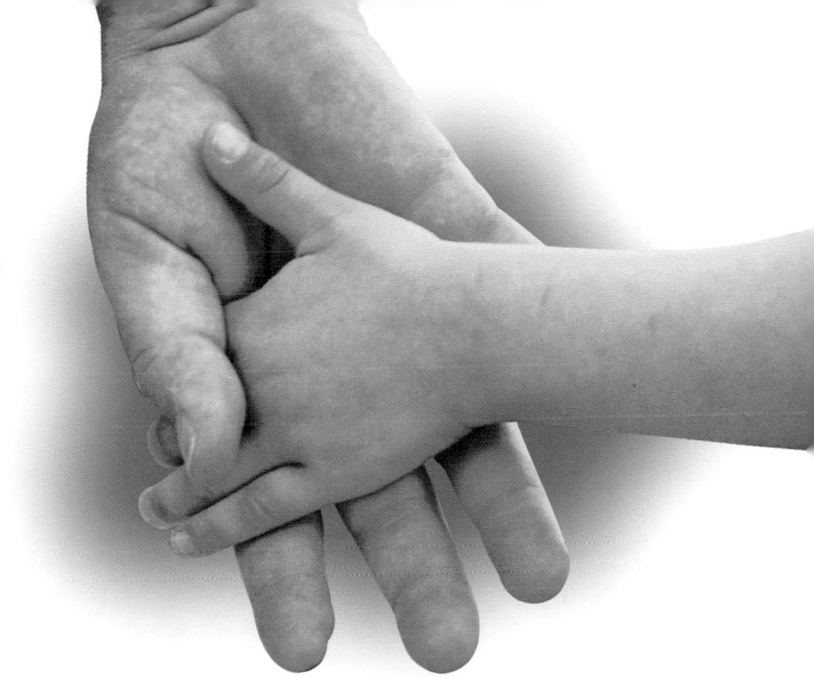

Your hands can say, "I love you."

You can use your hands to create a piece of art.

bright sunshine, brush away flies, and "catch" you when you fall.

You have five toes on each foot. Your feet can do some of the things your hands can do. You can use your feet to touch and feel things. And if you try, you can even pick up and hold things with your toes. It takes practice!

Your feet also do things your hands can't do. Your feet support the weight of your body so that you can stand, walk, run, skate, and jump. Your feet are especially good for dancing and kicking a ball.

Why Do You Have Nails?

Do you know why you have fingernails and toenails? They help protect the ends of your fingers and toes.

Your fingernails and toenails are made of strong stuff called **keratin** (KEHR uh tihn). Keratin is made up of hard skin. Animal claws, hoofs, and horns also are made of keratin. Animals use these for protection, too.

The outer skin at the base of your nail is called the cuticle (KYOO tuh kuhl). Your nails grow from the cuticle. As this layer

People and many animals have nails, hoofs, or claws to protect their fingers or toes.

of skin grows, it pushes the older skin forward to make the nail. Near the growing area, you cannot see the flow of blood as well as you can in the rest of the nail. This is why you see a light half-moon at the base of your nails.

Your nails grow all the time. You need to cut them or file them when they get too long. Otherwise, they may scratch you, split and break, or catch on things. It is a good idea to clip your toenails straight across so that they will not dig into the skin at the corners of your toes.

This picture shows the inside of a toe. The nail grows from a layer of skin below the base of the nail.

nail
growing layer
bone

Your Very Own Marks

Press your finger on a window or a mirror. Can you see your fingerprint? No one in the world has fingerprints exactly like yours. Your footprints are different from everyone else's, too.

Take a close look at your fingertips. See the many tiny lines going this way and that way? These lines form designs with loops, waves, and circles. Each finger has a different design. You have 10 fingers and 10 different fingerprints.

When you were born, the doctors probably made a copy of your footprint. It may be on your birth certificate. Newborn babies in hospitals look a lot alike, but all their footprints are different. The millions of children in the world have millions of fingerprints and footprints. Now you know, though, that the marks made by your fingers and your feet are yours alone.

Picture Yourself

TRY THIS! 2

Here is your chance to tell everyone all about you!

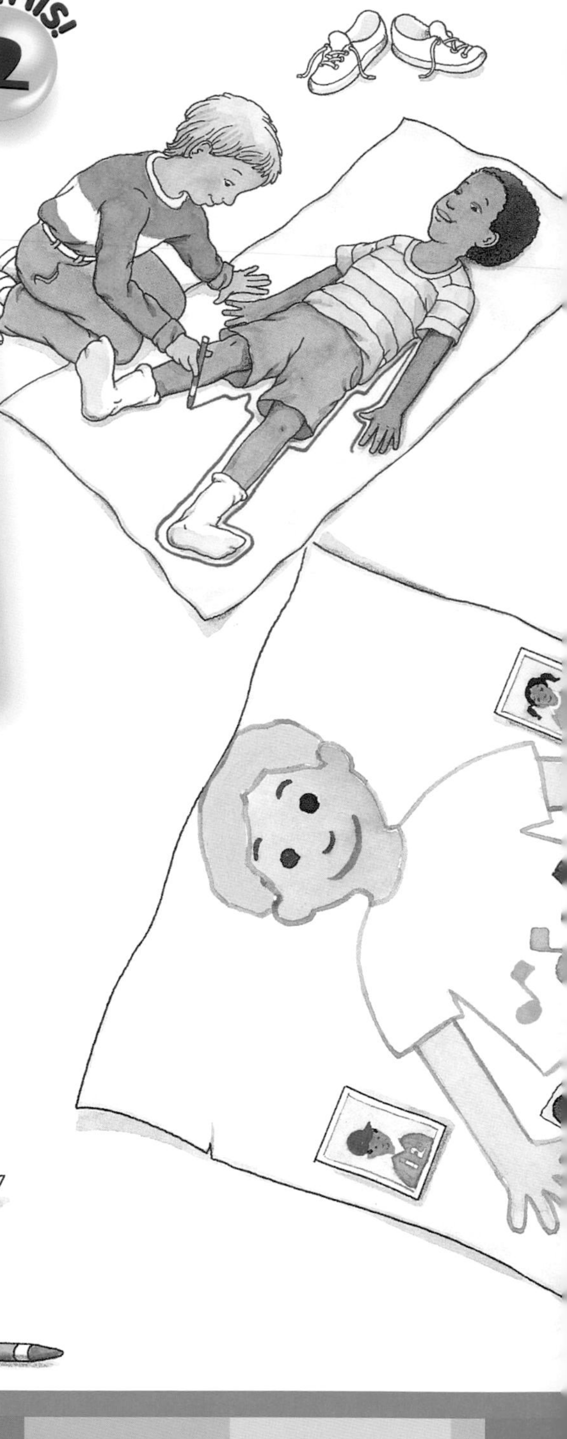

You Will Need:

a large sheet of butcher paper, at least as tall as you
crayons and markers
a friend or adult
a pen
photographs (get permission)
glue
old magazines (get permission)
scissors

What To Do:

1. Unroll the butcher paper onto a hard surface, such as a kitchen floor. If the ends roll up, place a heavy book on each of the four corners.

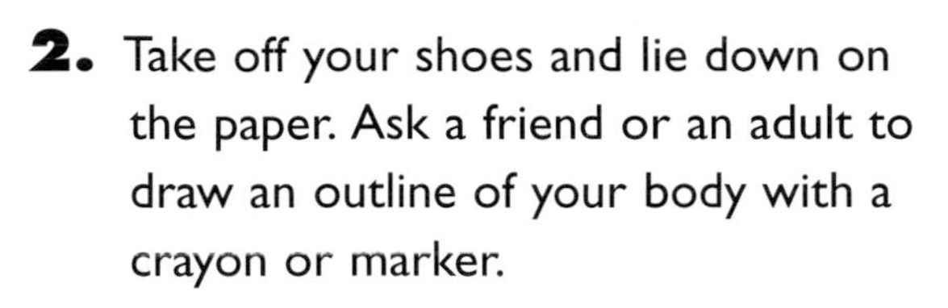

2. Take off your shoes and lie down on the paper. Ask a friend or an adult to draw an outline of your body with a crayon or marker.

3. Cover the paper with all sorts of information about yourself. Write both inside and outside the outline. Include your name, birthday, age, eye color, and hair color. Name your friends and hobbies. List things you like or don't like.

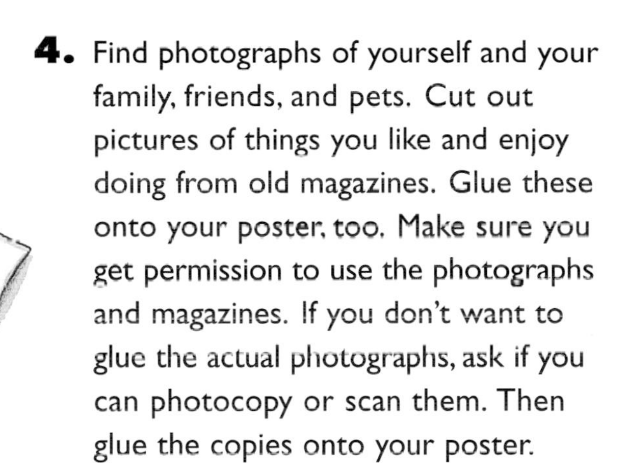

4. Find photographs of yourself and your family, friends, and pets. Cut out pictures of things you like and enjoy doing from old magazines. Glue these onto your poster, too. Make sure you get permission to use the photographs and magazines. If you don't want to glue the actual photographs, ask if you can photocopy or scan them. Then glue the copies onto your poster.

Hang this poster on your bedroom wall or closet door. Make a new poster every year to see how you have changed.

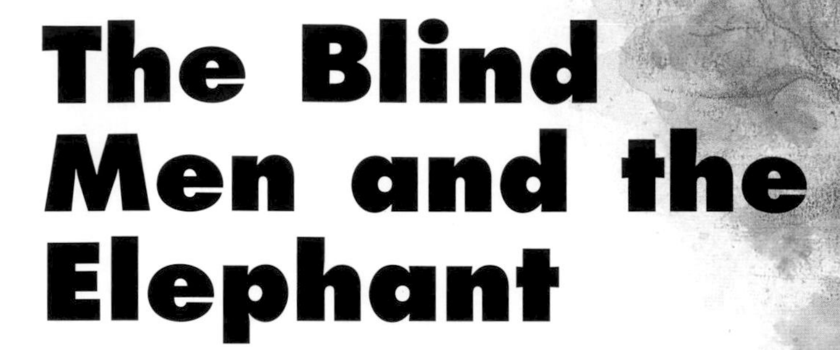

The Blind Men and the Elephant

No one can know all about you just by looking at the different parts of you. Read this fable from India to find out how six blind men learned this lesson.

Long ago in India, six blind men lived together. They had heard about elephants often, but they had never seen one.

The blind men lived near the palace of a Rajah (RAH juh). The Rajah was the ruler of all the people. At the palace of the Rajah, there were many elephants.

"Let us go to the palace of the Rajah," said one blind man. "We can learn about elephants there."

"Yes, let us go," said the others.

It was a hot day, but the six blind men walked to the palace. They walked one behind the other. The smallest blind man was the leader.

The second blind man put his hand on the shoulder of the leader. Each blind man put his hand on the shoulder of the man in front of him.

A friend of the six blind men met them at the palace. He led them to an elephant that was standing in the courtyard.

The first blind man put out his hand and touched the side of the elephant. "How smooth!" he said. "An elephant is like a wall."

The second blind man put out his hand and touched the trunk of the elephant. “How round!” he said. “An elephant is like a snake.”

The third blind man put out his hand and touched the tusk of the elephant. “How sharp!” he cried. “An elephant is like a spear.”

The fourth blind man put out his hand and touched the leg of the elephant. “How tall!” he said. “An elephant is like a tree.”

The fifth blind man put out his hand and touched the ear of the elephant. "How wide!" he called out. "An elephant is like a fan."

The sixth blind man put out his hand and touched the tail of the elephant. "How thin!" he cried. "An elephant is like a rope."

Then the friend of the six blind men led them into a garden. It was a hot day. "Wait here. I will bring you water to drink," he said. "You must not go out in the sun again until you rest."

The six blind men sat down in the shade of a big tree. They talked about the elephant. "An elephant is like a wall," said the first blind man.

"A wall?" said the second blind man. "You're wrong. An elephant is like a snake."

"A snake?" said the third blind man. "You're wrong. An elephant is like a spear."

"A spear?" said the fourth blind man. "You're wrong. An elephant is like a tree."

"A tree?" said the fifth blind man. "You're wrong. An elephant is like a fan."

"A fan?" said the sixth blind man. "You're wrong. An elephant is like a rope."

The six blind men could not agree. Each man shouted,

"A wall!"

"A snake!"

"A spear!"

"A tree!"

"A fan!"

"A rope!"

The friend came back with water to drink. At the same time, the Rajah was awakened by the shouting. He looked out and saw the six blind men below him in the garden.

"Stop!" the Rajah called out.

The six blind men stopped shouting. They knew that the Rajah was a wise man. They listened to him. The Rajah spoke in a kind voice. "The elephant is a big animal. Each man touched only one part. You must put all the parts together to find out what an elephant is like."

The six blind men listened. They drank the cool water, as they rested in the shade. They talked quietly.

"The Rajah is right," they said. "Each one of us knows only a part. To find out the whole truth we must put all the parts together."

The six blind men walked out of the courtyard. The smallest blind man led the way. The second blind man put his hand on the shoulder of the leader. Each blind man put his hand on the shoulder of the man in front. They walked home, one behind the other.

Inside of You

The outside of you is plain to see. But what is inside of you? You know there is blood inside, because sometimes you cut yourself and you bleed. You know there is a heart, because you can feel it beating. But what other things are inside, and how do they work together to let you move, think, and breathe?

The Building Blocks of Life

Your whole body is made up of cells.

Cells are the building blocks of life. Every living thing is made of cells. Plants are made of cells. Animals and people are made of cells, too. Even you are made of cells. Without cells, life could not exist. You could not exist.

The human body is made of more than a thousand or even a million cells. It takes many billions of cells to make a body. These cells are so small that you need a microscope to see them.

Cells come in different shapes and sizes. They do different jobs too. There are blood cells, skin cells, and muscle cells.

The same kinds of cells gather and work together to make **tissues** (TIHSH yooz). The different parts of your body are made of different tissues. Muscle cells come together to make muscles. Skin cells come together to make skin. Bone cells come together to make bones. Muscle, skin, and bone are different kinds of tissues.

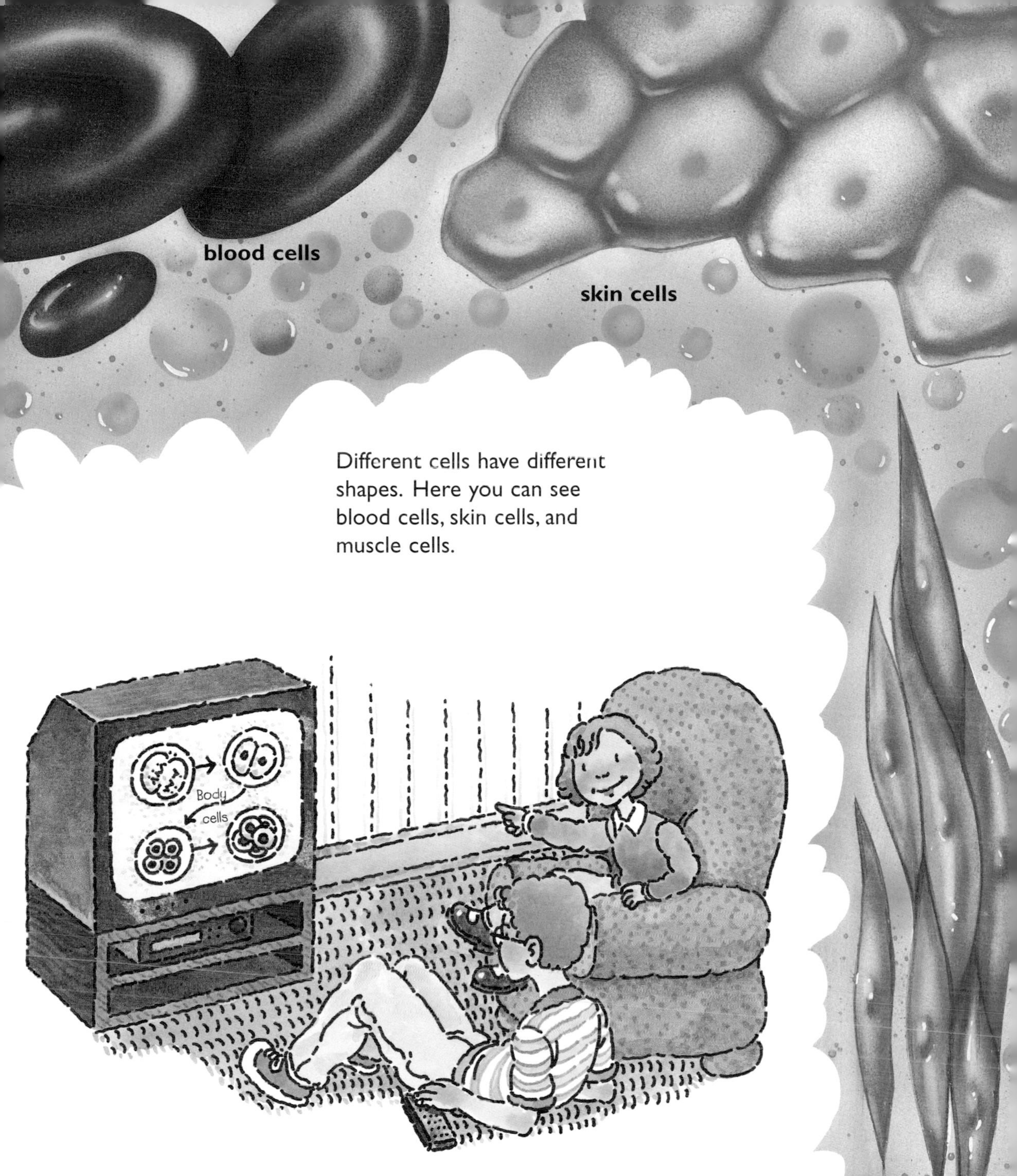

Different cells have different shapes. Here you can see blood cells, skin cells, and muscle cells.

Every minute, your body makes billions of new cells. Cells make new cells by growing and dividing in two. Then the two cells divide and become four cells. The four cells become eight cells. The dividing goes on and on. This is how your body grows.

muscle cells

Your Body's Framework

When you tap the top of your head do you feel something hard? When you tap the front of your leg, is it also hard? What you're feeling are bones.

Your body has bones of many shapes and sizes. Your leg bones are big and long. The bones of your fingers and toes are small and short. The bones of your skull, kneecaps, and shoulder blades are flat. Your rib bones are rounded. Some of your bones, such as those in your face, have very odd shapes.

Together, your bones make up the **skeleton** (SKEHL uh tuhn) inside you. You have probably seen a skeleton before. People like to hang up plastic ones on Halloween. Your skeleton grows with you and gives shape to your body. If you did not have a skeleton, you would flop around like a rag doll.

TRY THIS! 1

Hundreds of bones make up your skeleton. Some of the bones are shown on the next page with their common names. Can you feel these bones in your body?

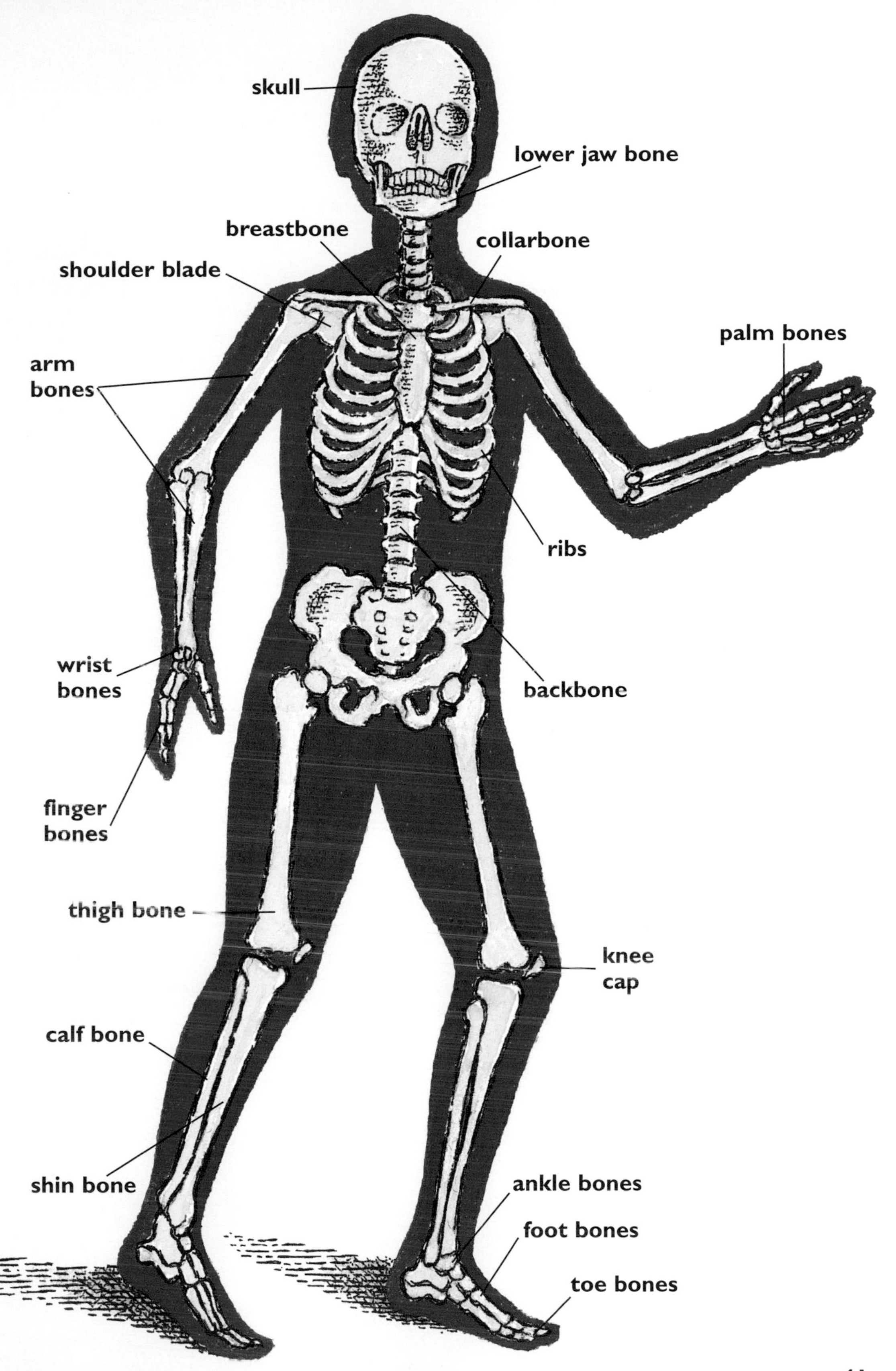
skull
lower jaw bone
breastbone
collarbone
shoulder blade
palm bones
arm
bones
ribs
wrist
bones
backbone
finger
bones
thigh bone
knee
cap
calf bone
shin bone
ankle bones
foot bones
toe bones

Are you bending your arms or legs as you read this page? Where your arm or leg is bending is where two or more bones meet. Bones come together at places called **joints** (joynts). Some joints, like those in the skull, do not move. Other joints, like those in the legs, do move. You have joints in your arms, jaws, shoulders, hips, wrists, ankles, fingers, and toes. Your bones and joints work together to help you move around. They help you to shoot a basketball, run, walk, and jump.

Your hand has many joints. It can bend in many places.

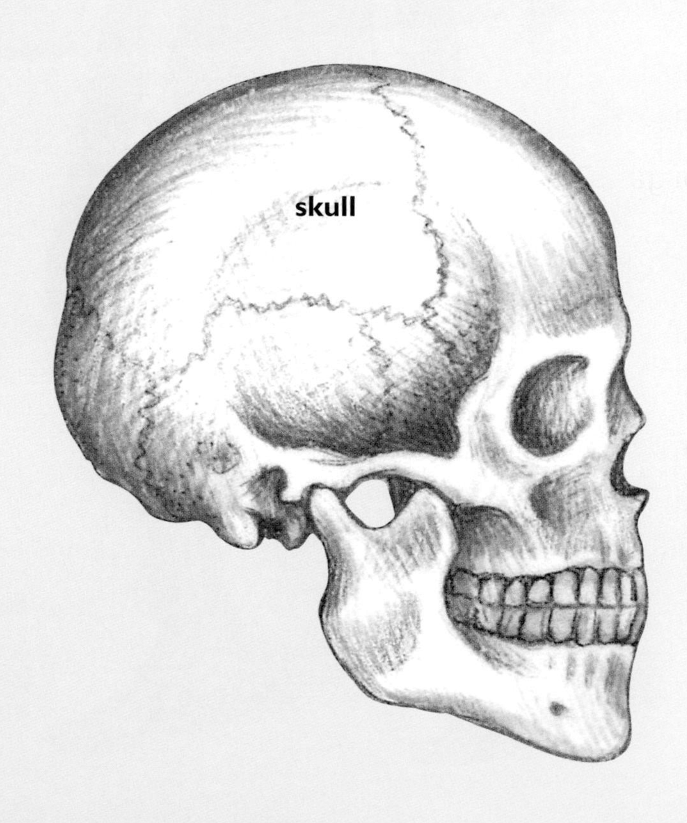

KNOW It All!

The smallest bones in your body are the stirrup bones. You have a stirrup bone in each ear. Each one is about 1/10 inch (0.25 cm) long.

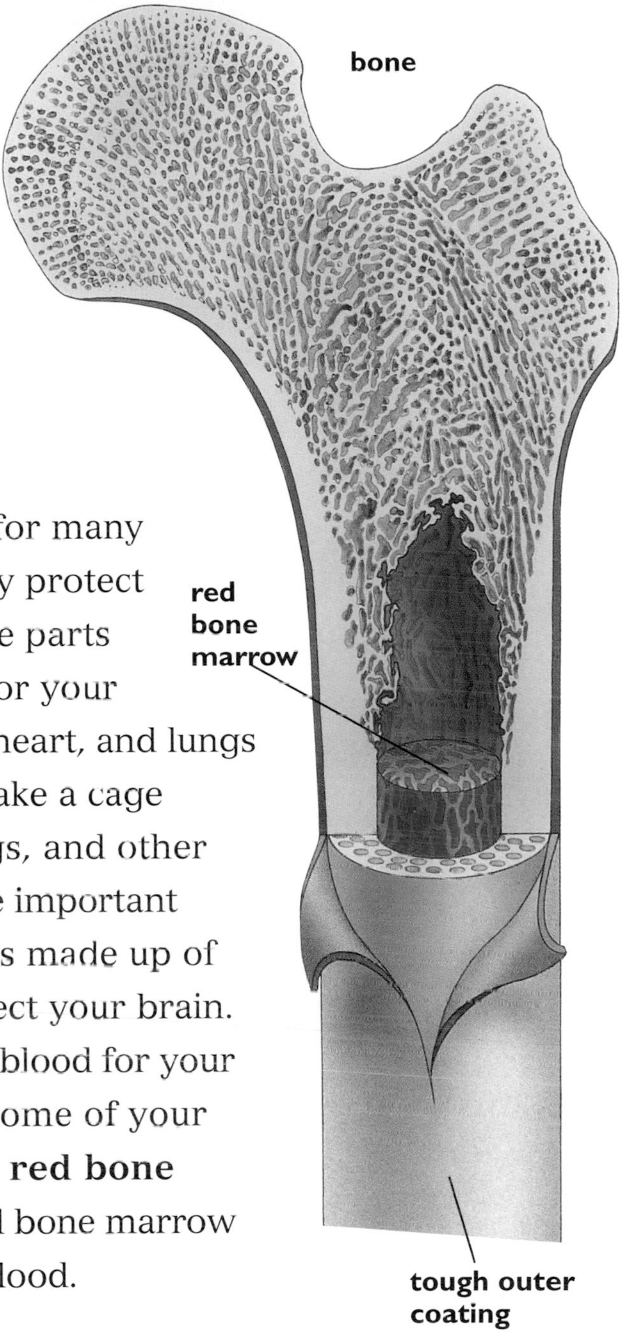

Bones are important for many reasons. First of all, they protect your organs. Organs are parts of you that work hard for your body. Your brain, eyes, heart, and lungs are organs. Your ribs make a cage around your heart, lungs, and other organs. They keep these important organs safe. Your skull is made up of many bones. They protect your brain.

Bones also help make blood for your body. In the center of some of your bones is a liquid called **red bone marrow** (MAR oh). Red bone marrow helps your body make blood.

Amazing Muscles

Your skeleton is covered with muscles. In fact, you have more than 600 muscles in your body.

Some of your muscles are connected to bones. These muscles help you move. Your leg muscles help you run and skip. Your arm muscles help you lift and carry things. The muscles in your face help you laugh, speak, blink, and make funny faces. Your tongue is made up of muscles, too. It helps

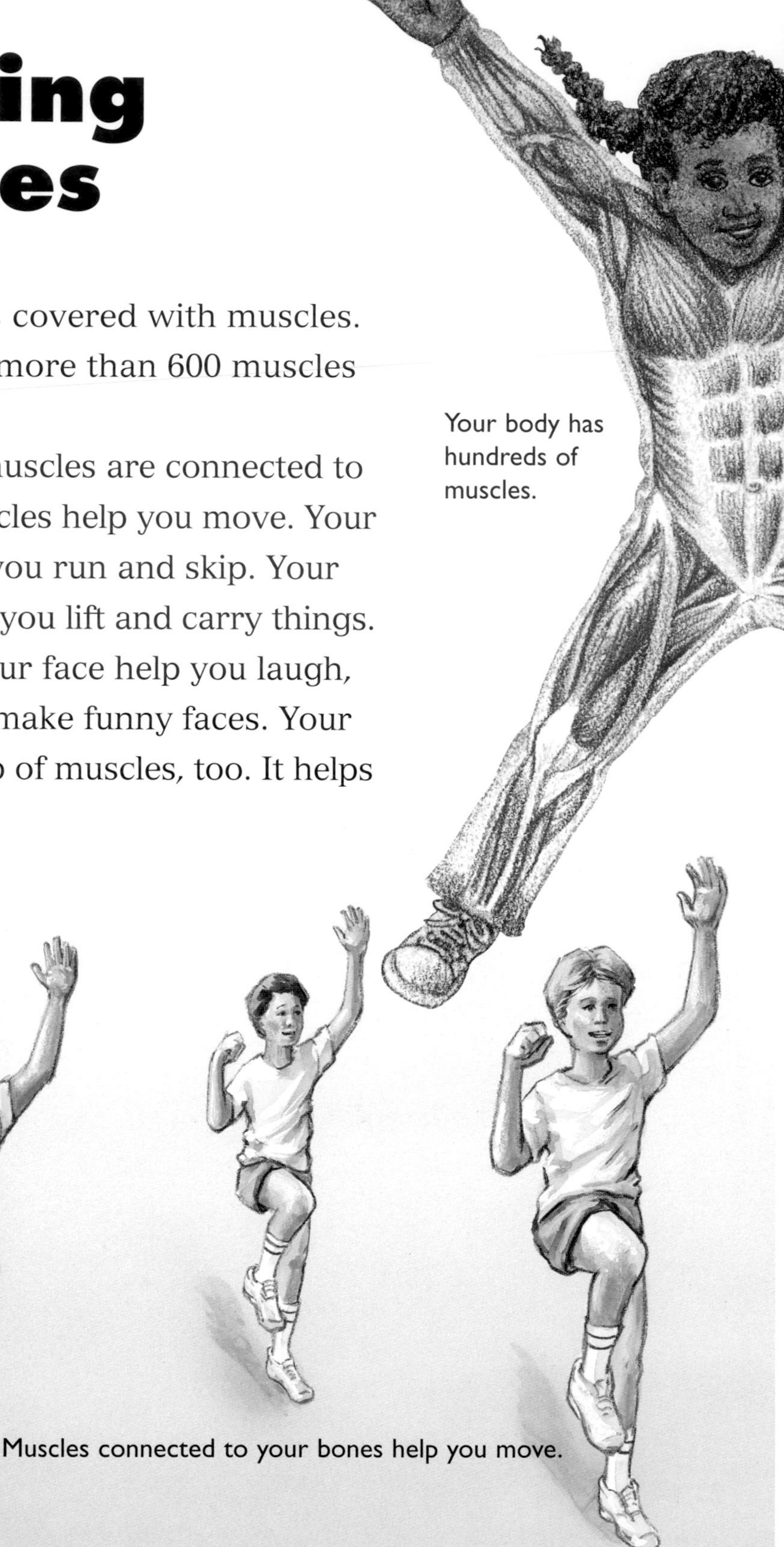

Your body has hundreds of muscles.

Muscles connected to your bones help you move.

you chew and swallow. Muscles in your chest help air move in and out of your body.

Some of your big hard-working muscles are joined to your bones by strong, tough cords called **tendons** (TEHN duhnz). You can feel a tendon on the back of your ankle. This tendon connects the muscles in your lower back leg, or calf, to your heel.

KNOW It All!

Muscles often work in pairs. The muscle in the front of your upper arm is your biceps. The muscle in the back of your upper arm is your triceps. Your biceps bend your arm and your triceps straighten it.

Some muscles are not fastened to bones. For example, muscles in your throat, stomach, and intestines help move food through your body. Your heart is a muscle. It helps pump blood through your body.

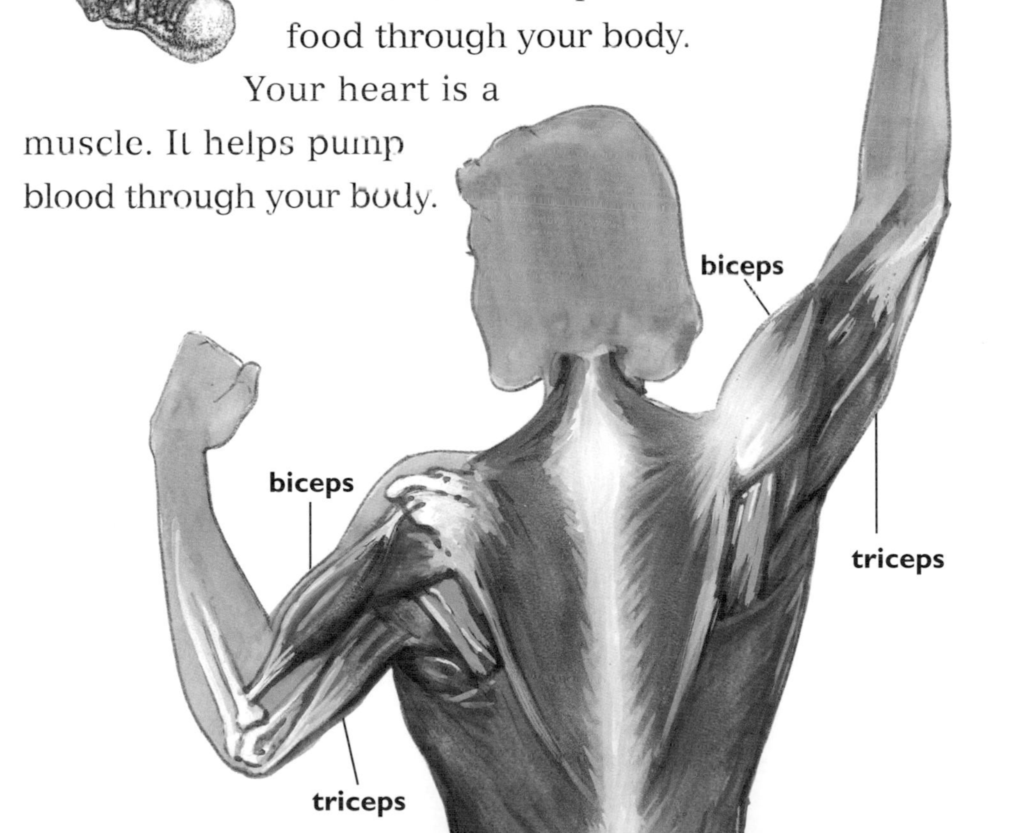

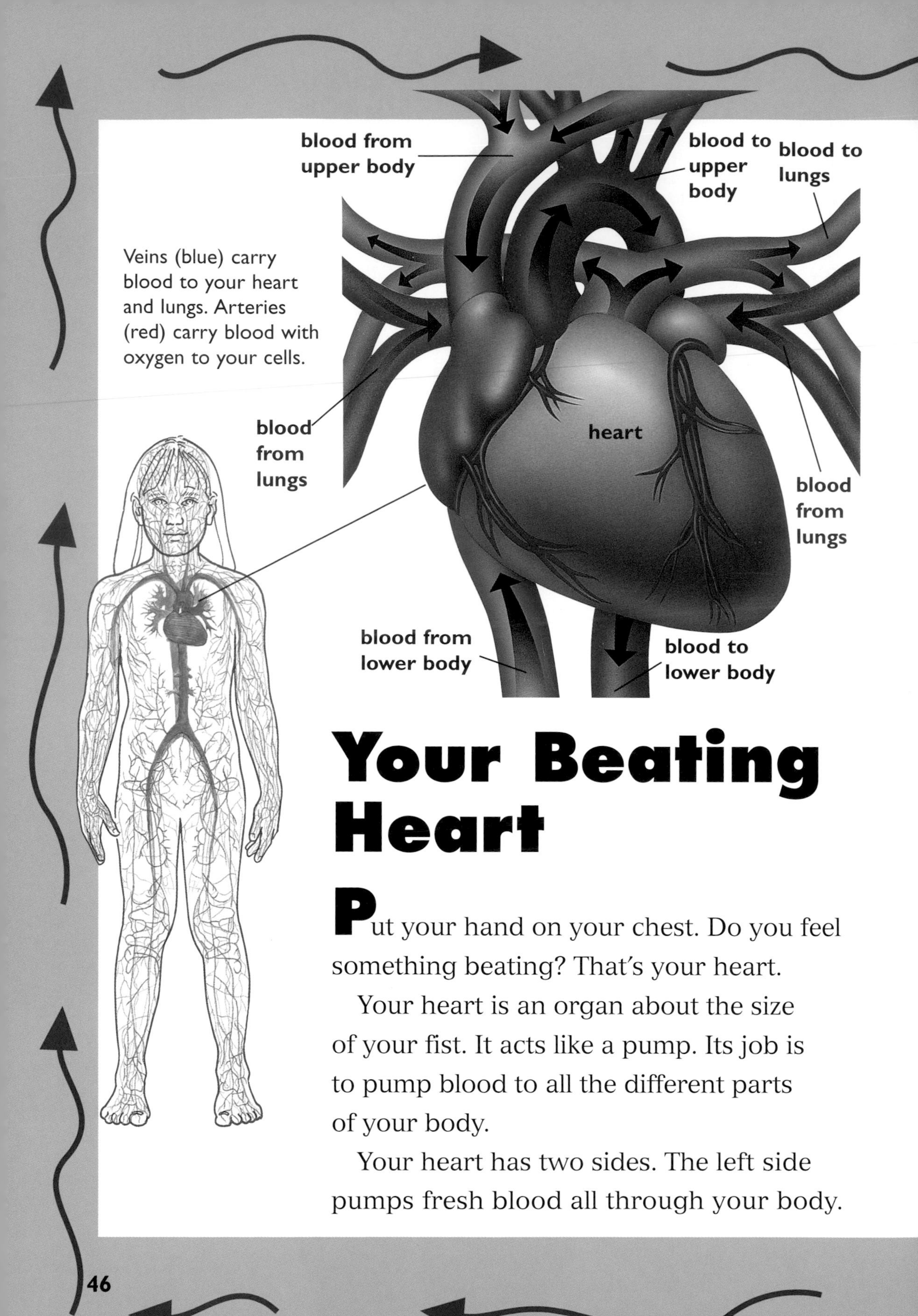

Veins (blue) carry blood to your heart and lungs. Arteries (red) carry blood with oxygen to your cells.

Your Beating Heart

Put your hand on your chest. Do you feel something beating? That's your heart.

Your heart is an organ about the size of your fist. It acts like a pump. Its job is to pump blood to all the different parts of your body.

Your heart has two sides. The left side pumps fresh blood all through your body.

The blood travels through tubes called **arteries** (AHR tuh reez). This blood brings a gas called **oxygen** (AHK suh juhn) to your cells. Cells need oxygen to work. At the same time, this blood picks up wastes that your cells must get rid of. The blood comes back to your heart by way of different tubes, called **veins** (vaynz).

When the blood returns to your heart, it comes into the right side. Then it is pumped to your **lungs** (luhngz).

You have two lungs in your chest. They are the organs that help you breathe. In the lungs, the blood gets rid of wastes and picks up more oxygen. Now it is fresh again. The blood is pumped back to the left side of your heart, ready to restart its journey. Blood leaving your heart right now will travel to your toes and back again in about one minute.

TRY THIS! 1

Want to know how fast your heart beats? Check your pulse. You can feel how fast your blood is being pushed through the arteries in your wrist. Place your first two fingers on the thumb side of the inside of your wrist. Can you feel your pulse? Count it for 60 seconds (1 minute). The number you come up with is your pulse rate. Do 25 jumping jacks. Check your pulse again. Did it change? Check your pulse again after resting for a few minutes. How has it changed now?

What Does Blood Do?

Chances are you have cut yourself at one time or another. What happened? Did you bleed? If so, you know what blood looks like. Do you know why your body needs blood?

Blood brings oxygen and **nutrients** (NOO tree uhnts) to your cells. Every cell in your body needs these things. At the same time, your blood takes wastes from your cells. Every cell in your body makes wastes.

Blood has three kinds of cells: red cells, white cells, and platelets (PLAYT lihts).

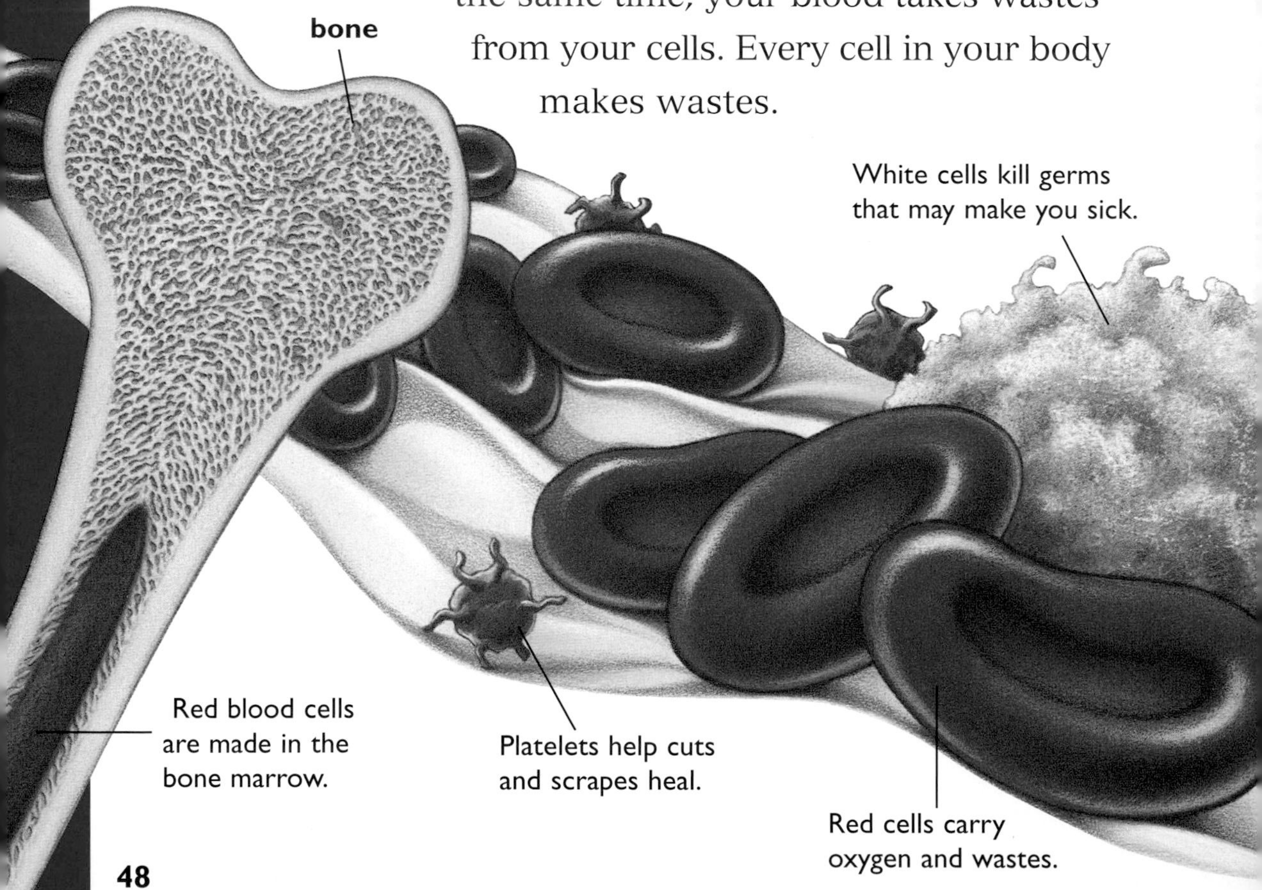

Blood helps your body in other ways, too. Blood helps keep your body at a certain temperature. Different kinds of cells in your blood fight to make you better when you are sick.

Your body holds about 2.5 quarts (2.4 liters) of blood. That's a little more than half a 1-gallon (3.8-liter) milk container. Adults may have 5 quarts (4.7 liters) or more. When you cut yourself and lose some blood, your body makes new blood to take its place.

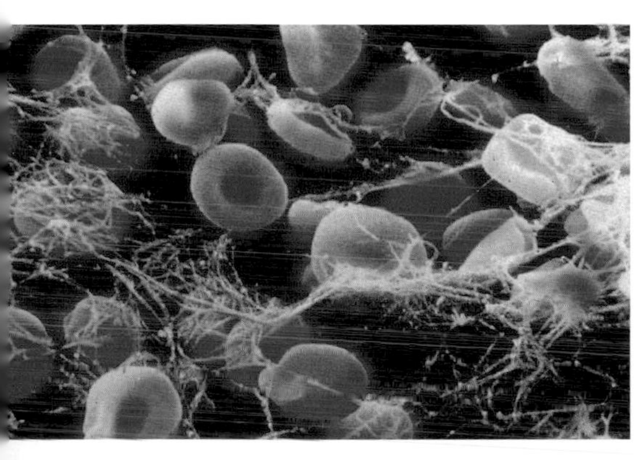

red blood cells

KNOW It All!

Blood is not always bright red. When blood mixes with oxygen, it turns bright red. But it turns a dark brownish-red after it drops off oxygen to the cells. This is why the veins under your skin do not look red. The color of your skin makes them look almost blue. When you cut yourself, your blood mixes with oxygen in the air and turns bright red.

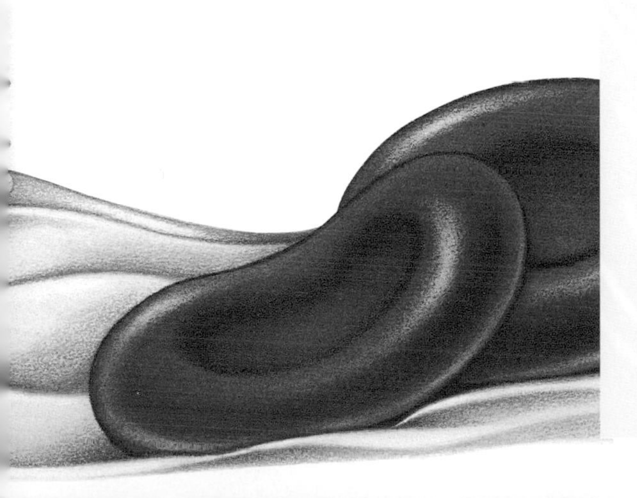

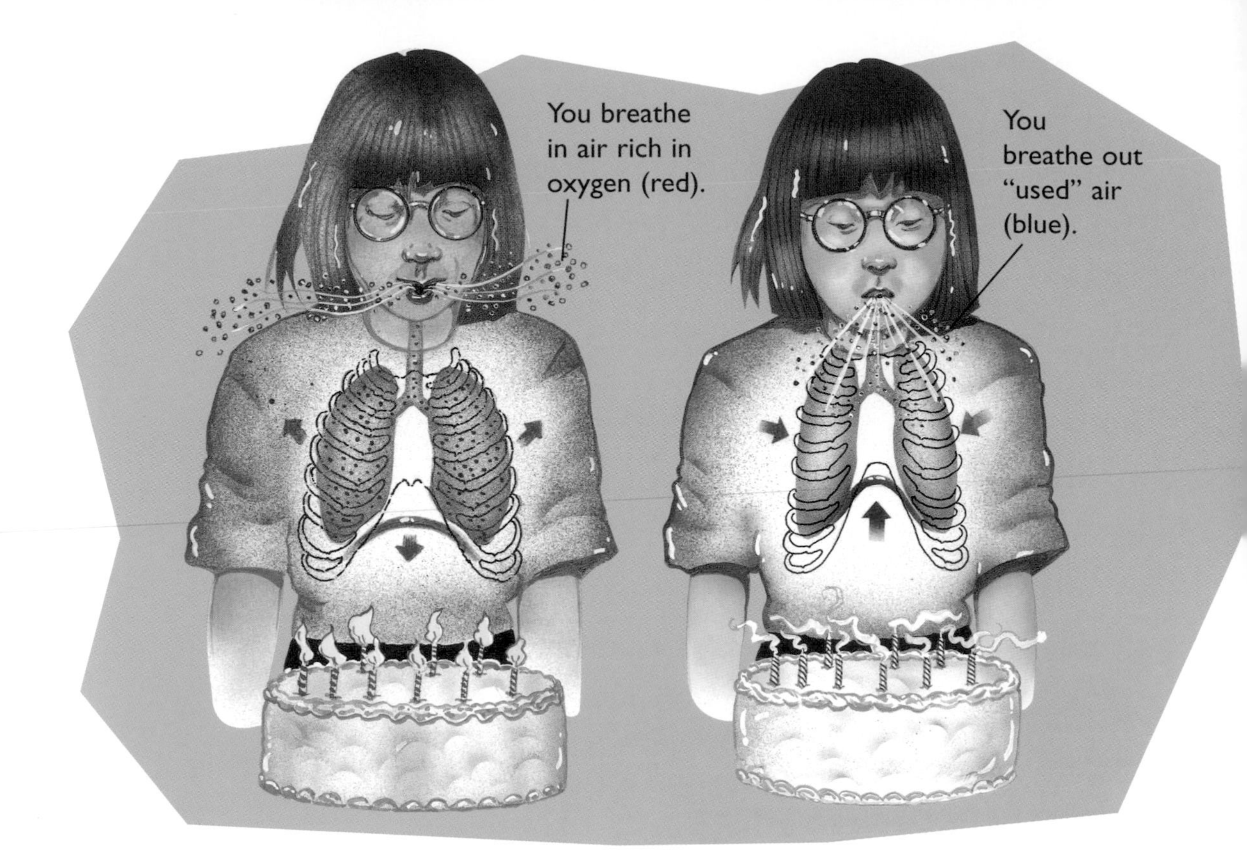

Every Breath You Take

You are always breathing. You do not even have to work at it. Your brain is in control.

Many things happen when you breathe. To begin with, air goes into your nose and mouth. There, the air warms up. Little hairs in your nose catch dust or dirt. The wetness in your nose also catches many of the germs you breathe in. Germs are tiny living things that can make you sick.

The air you breathe in has oxygen in it. Your body needs oxygen to live. The warm, clean air with oxygen goes down a tube called the **trachea** (TRAY kee uh). Two smaller tubes called bronchial (BRAHNG kee uhl) tubes bring the air from the trachea to the lungs. Your lungs keep your body supplied with oxygen.

Below your lungs is a muscle called the **diaphragm** (DY uh fram). Your diaphragm and the muscles attached to your ribs move your chest in and out. When your chest moves out, fresh air with oxygen fills your lungs. Blood flowing into the lungs picks up oxygen and leaves wastes behind. When you breathe out, you push the "used" air out of your body.

KNOW It All!

Bronchitis is an illness in the lining of the lungs' air passages. Bronchitis causes the bronchial tubes to make too much of a sticky fluid called mucus. A person with bronchitis may have a fever, chest pain, and a cough that brings up mucus. Often, medicine helps the person get better.

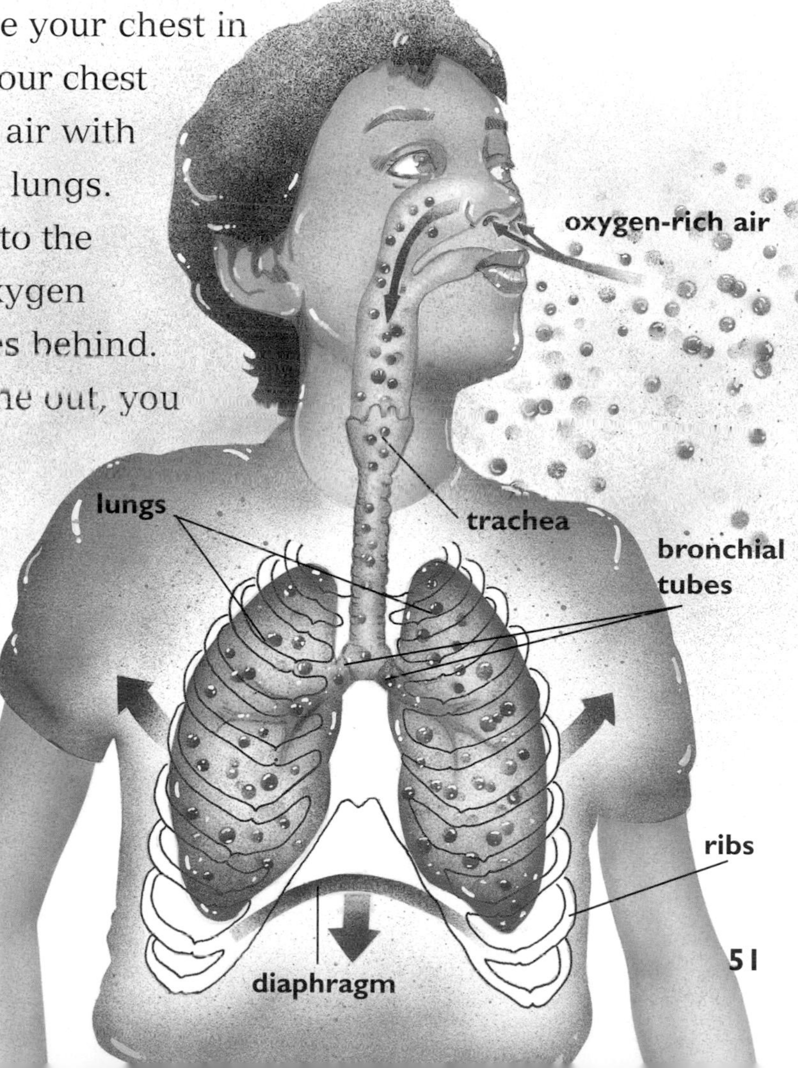

Many parts of your body work together to help you breathe.

What Happens When You Eat?

Eating good foods makes your body healthy.

You know which foods you love to eat. Have you ever wondered where those foods go after you eat them?

After you put food into your mouth, you begin to chew. As you chew, your teeth mash and grind the food into smaller pieces. While your teeth do their work, your tongue mixes the food with a liquid called **saliva** (suh LY vuh). Another word for saliva is spit. Saliva makes the food slippery and mushy. That makes it easier for you to swallow it. Your tongue then pushes the food to the back of your mouth and you swallow.

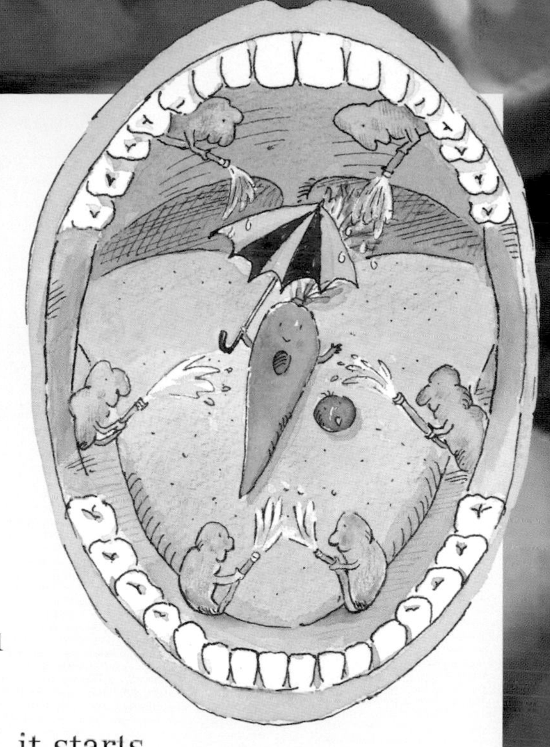

Glands produce the saliva, or spit, that makes your mouth wet. Your tongue mixes the saliva with your food. Saliva makes food easier to swallow.

Once you swallow your food, it starts on its way through your body. It travels from your mouth down a tube called the **esophagus** (ee SAHF uh guhs). By the time it takes to count to eight, the food is in your stomach. Here it will be changed so that your body can use it.

Eating juicy watermelon is a treat.

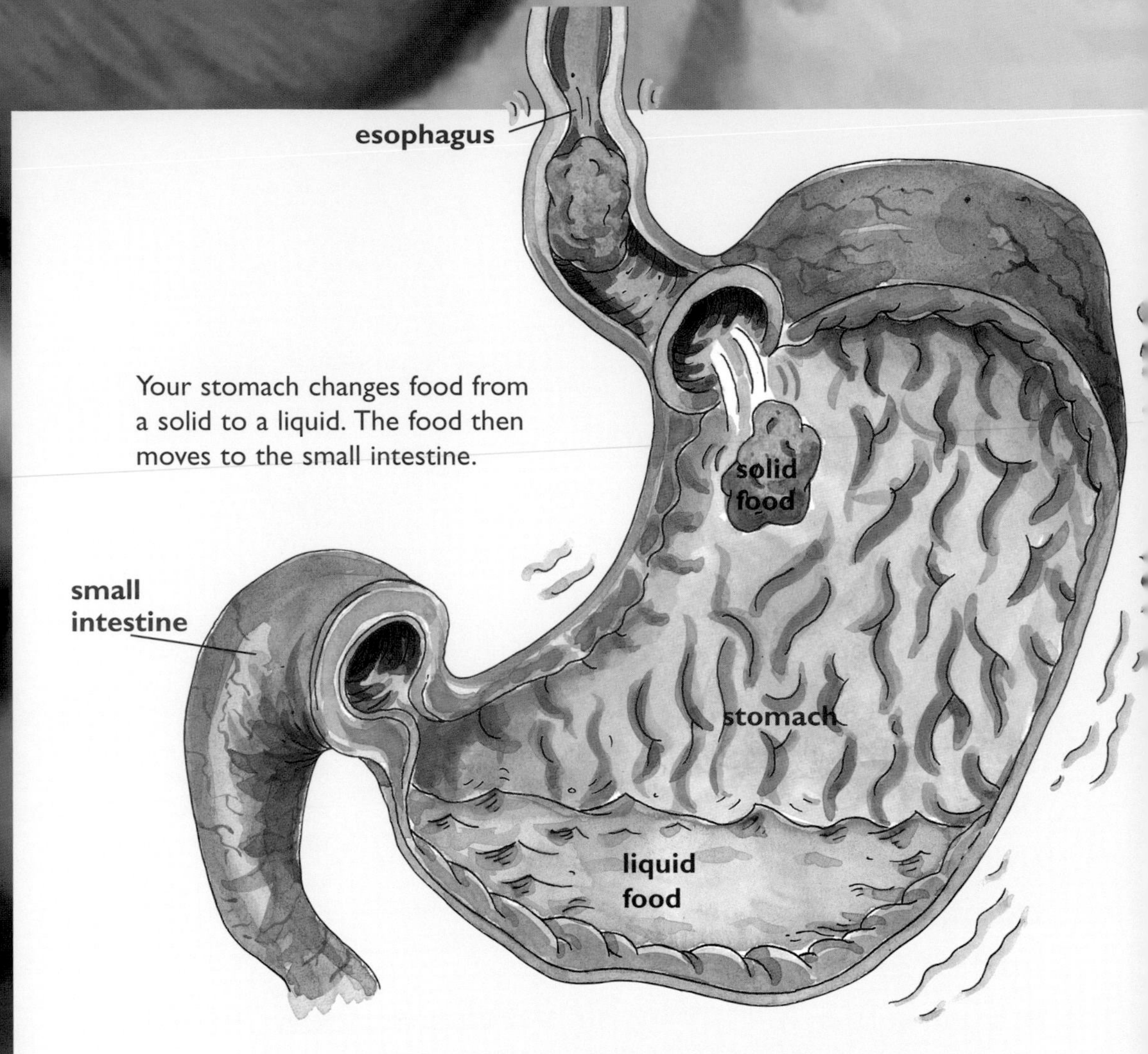

Your stomach continues the job your teeth began. It squeezes, mixes, mashes, and adds more liquids to the food. The food stays in your stomach for two to five hours. By the time it leaves your stomach, it is mostly liquid.

After the food leaves your stomach, it moves down into your small intestine (ihn TEHS tuhn). Here, powerful chemicals and a liquid called **bile** (byl) mix with the food and start to change it.

The food may stay in your small intestine for up to 40 hours. It is no longer what you ate, such as a hamburger or ice cream cone. It has been broken down, or digested, into very tiny pieces. The pieces are so small they can pass through tiny holes in the walls of the small intestine and into the blood. The blood carries the pieces into the cells. There, they help you grow and stay healthy.

The part of food that your body cannot use is called waste. It moves from the small intestine into another long tube called the large intestine. At the end of the large intestine is the rectum (REHK tuhm). This waste leaves your body through your rectum.

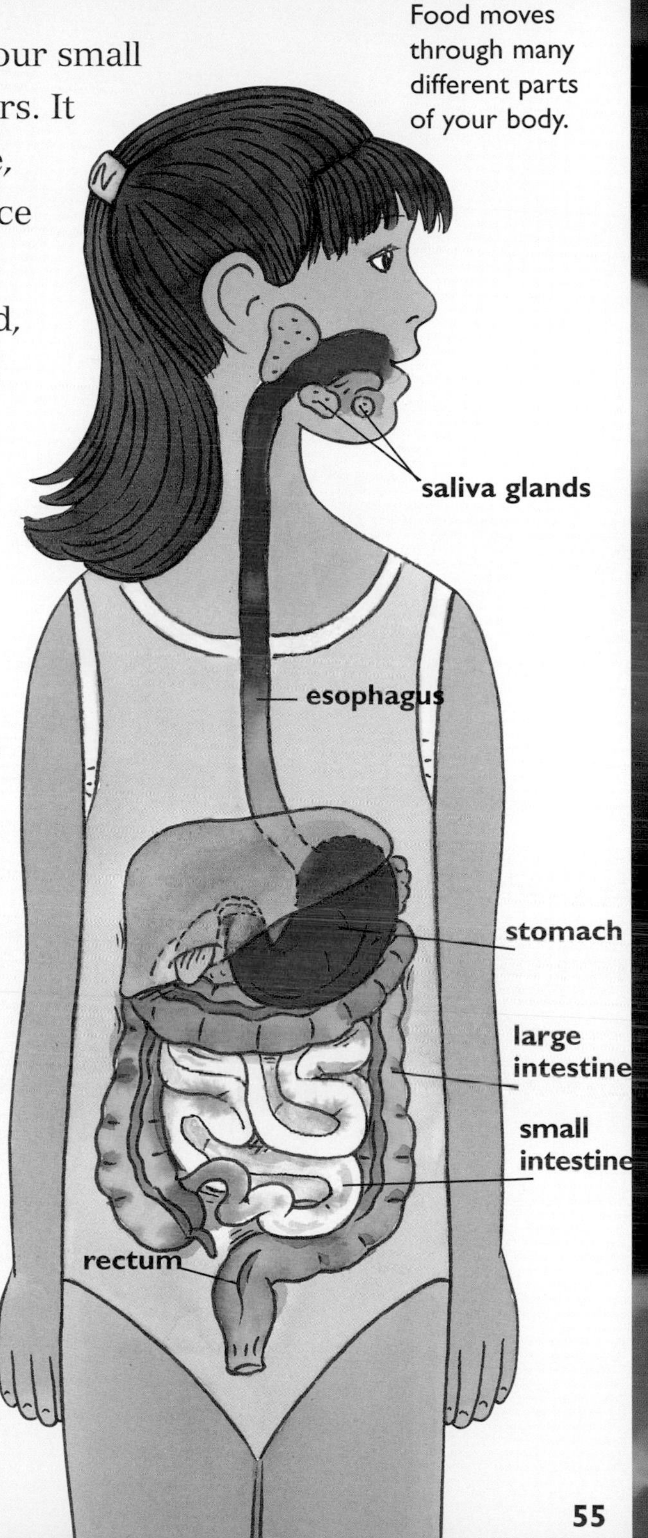

Food moves through many different parts of your body.

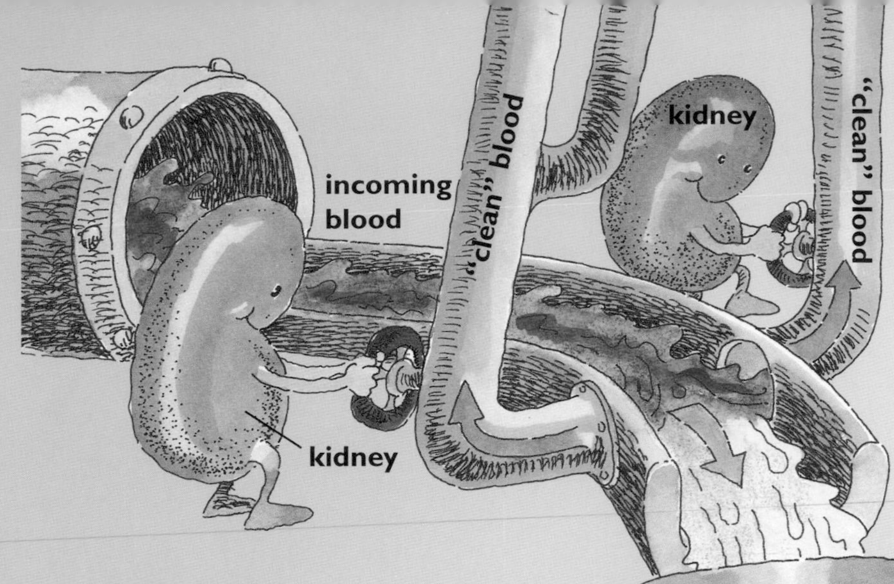

Keeping Blood Clean

In your back, just below your ribs and on each side of your spine, are your **kidneys**. You have two kidneys. They are each about as big as your heart. They are shaped like large beans.

Kidneys do an important job for your body. They help keep your blood clean.

Your blood takes wastes—things your body cannot use—away from your cells. On its way to your heart, the blood passes through your kidneys, and your kidneys take the waste materials out of the blood.

Your kidneys then get rid of this waste. They do this by making a liquid called **urine** (YUHR uhn). Urine leaves your

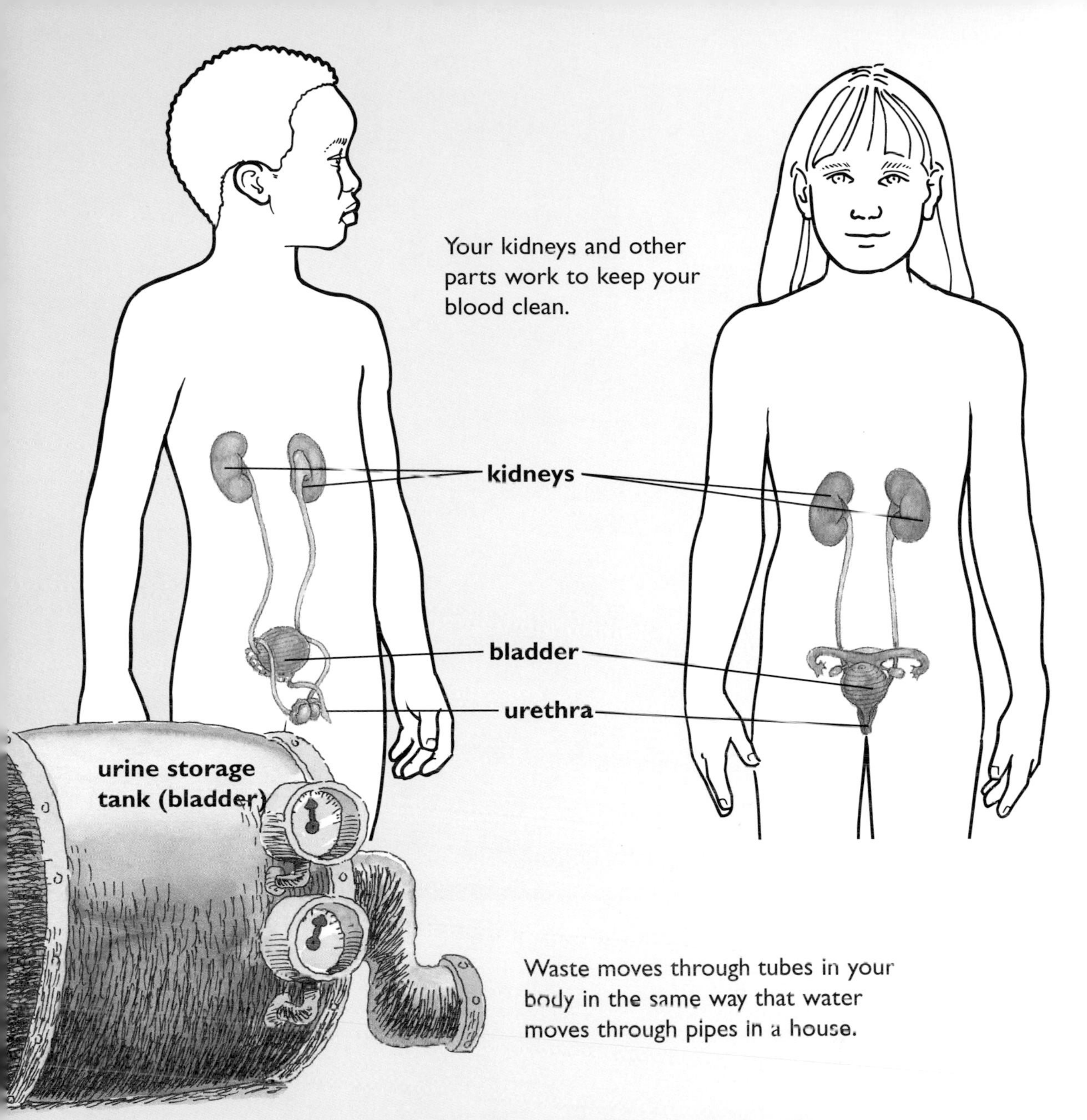

kidneys through two tubes and travels to a urine storage tank, the **bladder** (BLAD uhr).

Your bladder is a stretchy bag made of thin sheets of muscle. When it is full, you feel as if you need to use the bathroom. When you do, the bladder squeezes the urine out through a tube called the **urethra** (yoo REE thruh).

You can see the differences between boys and girls more and more as they grow older.

Boys and Girls Are Different

All bodies work the same in many ways. But as you know, there are some differences between boys and girls. These differences help make new life begin.

Girls have two small organs called **ovaries** (OH vuh reez). The ovaries lie inside the body near the hips. They hold tiny eggs. When an egg leaves one of the ovaries, it may join with a sperm cell to start a new life. Below a girl's bellybutton, there is another organ called a **uterus** (YOO tuhr uhs). It is here that a woman's baby grows. When the baby is ready to be born, it comes out through the **vagina** (vuh JY nuh).

Boys have a **penis** (PEE nihs) and a soft sack of skin called a **scrotum** (SKROH tuhm). Inside the scrotum are two **testicles** (TEHS tuh kuhlz). The testicles make sperm cells. When a sperm cell joins with a female egg, a new life may begin.

Whether you are a girl or a boy, you may want to be a parent when you grow up. These organs will help make that possible.

KNOW It All!

The bodies of boys and girls change as they grow up to be men and women. But they don't all change at the same time or the same speed. Some boys and girls change faster or begin changing sooner than others. For a while, they may look older and more grown-up. But the same kinds of changes happen for everyone in time.

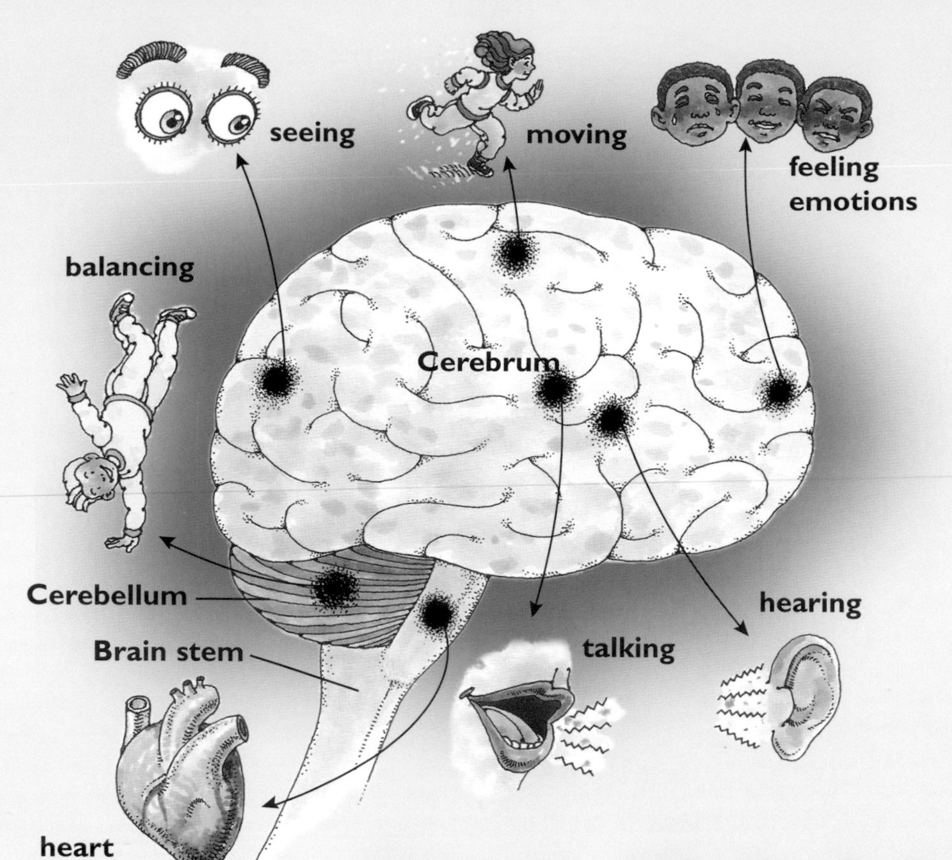

Your brain is made up of different parts. Each one allows you to do different things, such as seeing, moving, balancing, talking, or hearing.

Your Thinking Machine

You think, learn, and remember because you have a brain. You move because you have a brain. You feel, see, hear, and smell because you have a brain.

Your brain sits in your head, protected by your skull. Fluid inside your skull keeps your brain safe. It also gives your brain the nutrients it needs to work.

Your brain has three main parts. These are the cerebrum (SEHR uh bruhm), the cerebellum (sehr uh BEHL uhm), and the brain stem.

The cerebrum is the largest part. It receives messages about the world around you. For example, it tells you when something hurts. Then it tells your body what to do about those messages. When you feel pain, you may rub where it hurts.

The part of your brain called the cerebellum gives you the balance you need to ride a bike.

The cerebellum gives you balance. It makes sure the parts of your body work together so you can move around without falling down. For example, it helps you ride a bike.

The brain stem is important, too. It keeps your body running. It keeps your lungs breathing and your heart beating.

KNOW It All!

When you were born, your brain weighed less than 1 pound (0.45 kilogram). By the time you turn 6, your brain is nearly its full weight, about 3 pounds (1.3 kilograms).

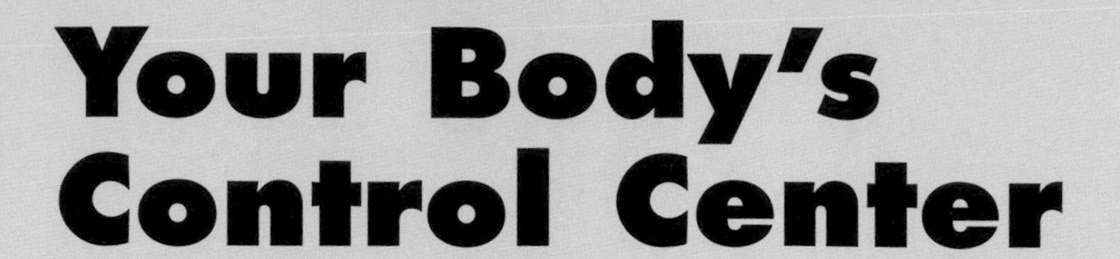

Your Body's Control Center

Your brain is the control center of your body. It is constantly receiving information about what is going on inside and outside your body. Your brain sorts this information very quickly and sends out messages that tell your body what to do.

Your brain sits at the upper end of your spinal cord. Your spinal cord is a thick rope of nerve cells. It begins at your neck and travels down your backbone. Messages between your

Nerves can carry messages up from your feet to your brain and back again more than 30 times in one second!

brain

Nerves in your fingers may tell your brain something is cold.

spinal cord

brain and the rest of your body travel through your spinal cord along nerve cells.

Your nerves are like tiny telephone wires. They lead from your spinal cord to your muscles and organs. Your body uses them to send messages to and from your brain. There are billions of nerve cells in your body.

Your nerves carry messages from your brain down your spinal cord. They may tell your hands to open a book or to turn a page. Your nerves also carry messages to your brain. If the book falls on your toe, your nerves will tell your brain, and you'll know your toe hurts!

Other nerves carry information to your brain from your eyes, ears, nose, and mouth. For example, you may know that a lemon is sour and that sugar is sweet. Nerves in your mouth tell your brain what they taste like.

TRY THIS! 1

See how well your friends can tell what something is just by gathering information from their hands, ears, and nose. Use a small cloth or paper bag as a "feelie bag." Put one small thing into the bag at a time, such as an apple, a pair of dice, or a feather. Have your friends take turns closing their eyes and putting a hand into the bag. Give each friend 10 seconds to feel, smell, and listen to the object. Can they guess what the object is?

Name That Body Part

Play this game with a friend. Pick one of the descriptions numbered 1 through 10 and read it out loud. Have your friend point to and name the body part described. Then have your friend pick and read a description for you.

1. Messages from all parts of your body come here. You need it to hear, see, smell, taste, feel, think, and learn.
2. Many of these are attached to your bones. They help you to move.
3. These catch sounds and send them to your brain.
4. These are found near your backbone. They are shaped like large beans. They clean your blood.
5. These give shape to your body and make it possible for you to stand and move. They also help protect your brain, heart, and other organs.
6. This has little hairs inside it that help clean the air you breathe in.
7. These pull oxygen into your body and push out used air.
8. This is a pump that works all day and all night. It moves your blood around your body.
9. This is where food goes after it leaves the esophagus.
10. These are places where bones come together. Without them, your body could not bend.

Answers: **1.** brain; **2.** muscles; **3.** ears; **4.** kidneys; **5.** bones; **6.** nose; **7.** lungs; **8.** heart; **9.** stomach; **10.** joints.

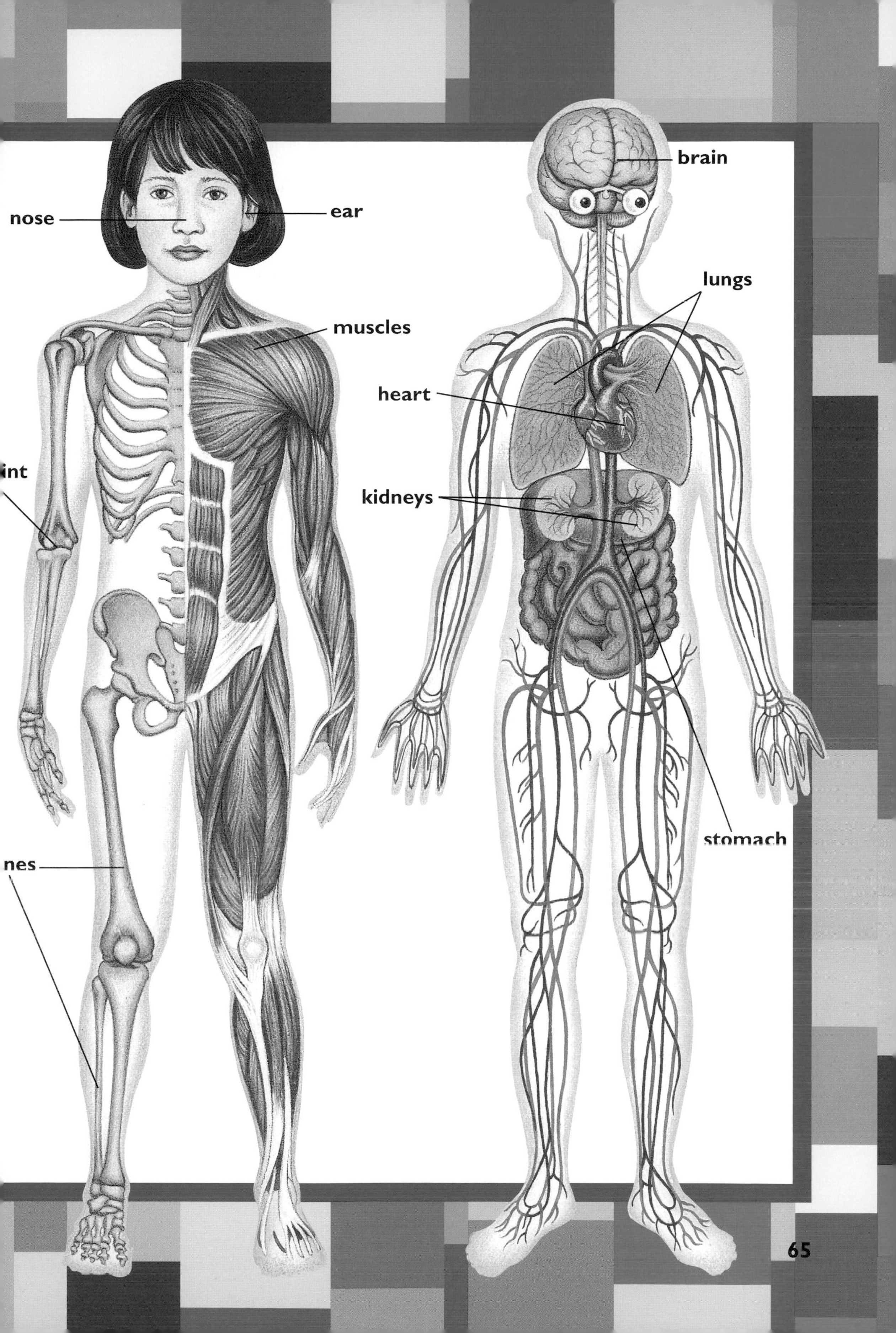
nose
ear
muscles
int
nes
brain
lungs
heart
kidneys
stomach

蘇皮波蘿捲
PINEAPPLE PASTRY
60 ¢

Your Senses

Senses are the powers you use to learn what is happening around you or inside you.

Some senses tell you about things outside your body. By hearing, seeing, touching, smelling, and tasting, you learn about the world.

Other senses tell you about changes that take place inside your body. They tell you when you are hungry, thirsty, tired, or hurting.

Whether they work inside or outside your body, senses can work alone or together to guide you and to guard you.

You use your eyes to see.

Each Sense Is Special

Think about the last time you were at the zoo. What did you see? Did you see a zebra? What did you smell? Were there any bad smells? What did you touch? Did you pet a goat? What did you hear? Did you hear the seals barking? Did you taste anything? Did you eat some peanuts or ice cream?

When you see, hear, touch, taste, and smell, you are using the five senses. You have other senses, too. Some of them are balance, hunger, pain, and thirst. They tell you when your body is standing, sitting, or

Your sense of taste allows you to enjoy your food.

hanging upside down. They also tell you when your body is moving and what it needs.

You have two groups of senses. One group tells you about things outside your body. It includes hearing, sight, smell, taste, and touch. It also tells you about heat, which is felt by special cells in your skin. These senses give you information about what is going on between your body and the outside world. When you touch something hot, they tell you to pull away.

The other group of senses tells you about the inside of your body. This group lets you know when you are hungry, thirsty, or tired—or when something hurts.

Your nose tells you about the smells around you.

You use your ears to hear the world around you.

Your sense of touch tells you if something feels soft or hard.

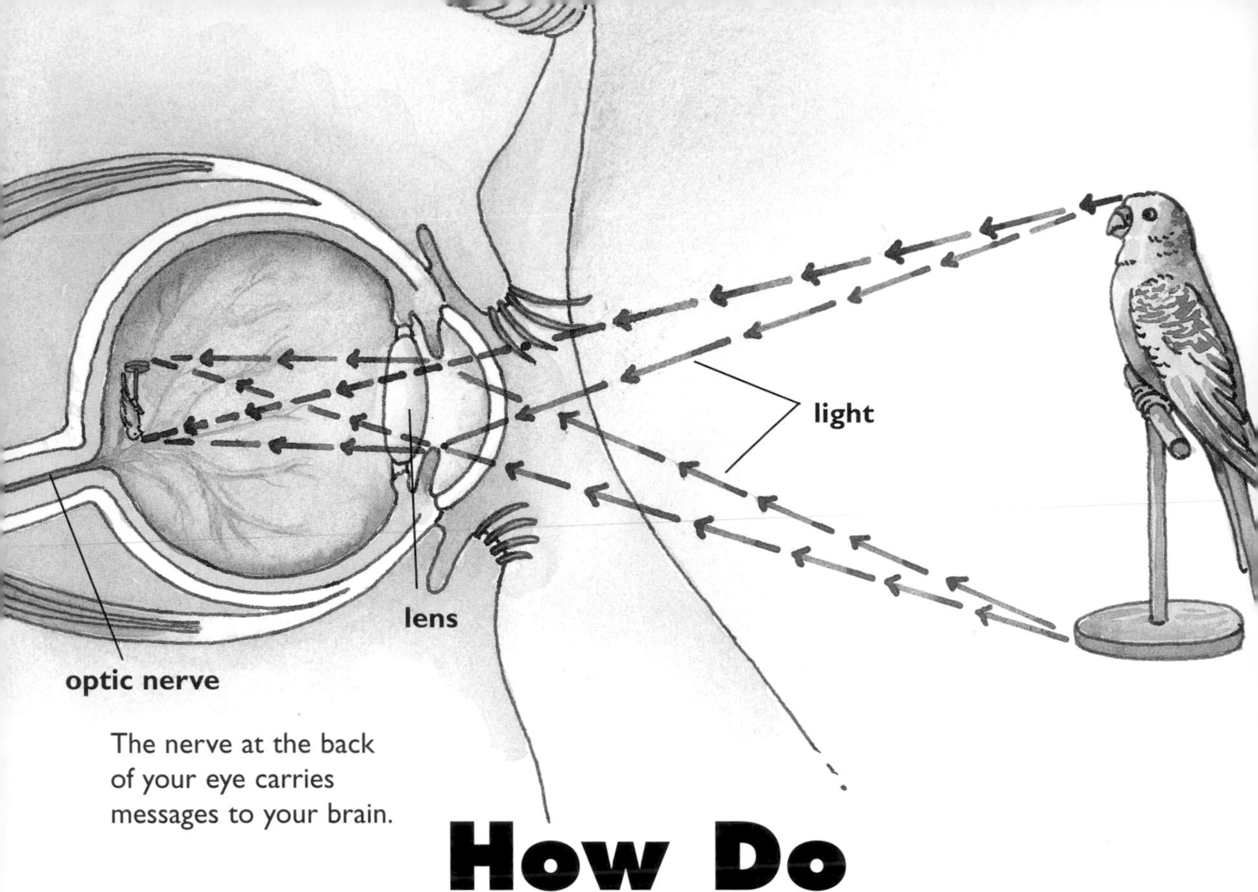

The nerve at the back of your eye carries messages to your brain.

How Do You See?

Sight may be your most important sense for finding out about the world around you. Your eyes work with your brain to help you see.

When you look at something, light bounces off it and enters your eye. The light travels to the back of your eye, to a nerve called the optic nerve. The optic nerve carries messages about the light to your brain. When your brain gets the messages, you know what you are seeing.

KNOW It All!

Tears come from little holes behind your eyelids. They bathe the outside of your eyeballs. They clear your eyes of dust and hairs. They also keep your eyes wet.

TRY THIS! 1

You can watch your pupils get bigger and smaller. It's easy. All you need is a lamp and a handheld mirror. Stand in a part of the room away from the lamp. Look at your pupils in the mirror. How big are they? Now stand close to the lamp. Look at your pupils again. How did they change? Did they get smaller? What do you think would happen if you moved away from the lamp again? Try it.

The colored circle on your eyeball is your iris. In the center of your iris is a dark spot. That is your pupil (PYOO puhl). Your pupil is a hole that lets light into your eye. Muscles in your iris make your pupil bigger or smaller to let in more or less light. The darker it is around you, the larger your pupil gets. The brighter it is around you, the smaller your pupil gets.

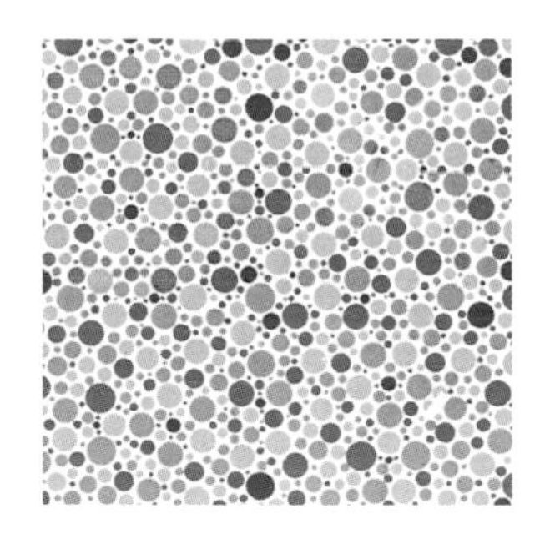

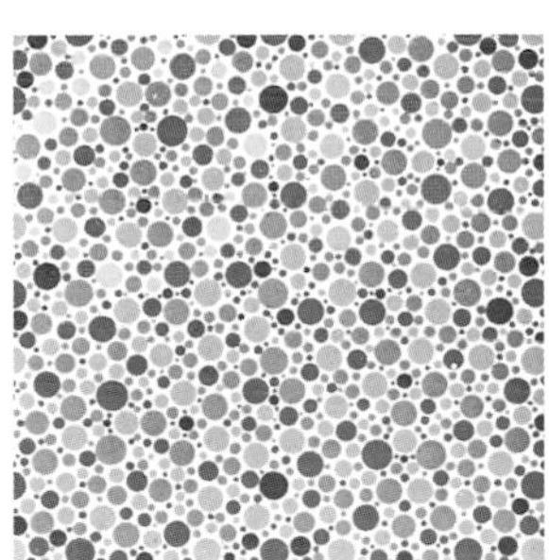

Some people cannot tell colors apart. They are color-blind. People who confuse blue and yellow may not see the O and X in the pattern at the far left. People who confuse red and green may not see the O and ▷ in the pattern at near left.

Some people wear glasses to help them see better.

When Eyes Need Help

Sometimes eyes need help to see well. When you go to your doctor for a checkup, he or she checks your eyes. You read a chart from across the room. If you cannot read the chart very well, your eyes might need help.

Eyeballs should be nearly round. People whose eyeballs are too long are near-sighted. Up close, they can see things well. But if they look at an object that is

In this picture, a far-off house looks clear.

If you are near-sighted, a far-off house looks blurry, like this.

If you are near-sighted, a clear picture does not form at the back of your eye.

The lens in a pair of eyeglasses will help you see clearly.

far away, such as a far-off house, they see a blur. That's because a clear picture of the house does not form at the back of their eyes. Near-sighted people wear glasses or contact lenses to help them see things that are far away.

People whose eyeballs are too short are far-sighted. They can see things in the distance well. But when they look at something nearby, such as the words in a book, they see a blur. A clear picture of the words does not form at the back of their eyes. Far-sighted people wear glasses or contact lenses to help them see things that are nearby.

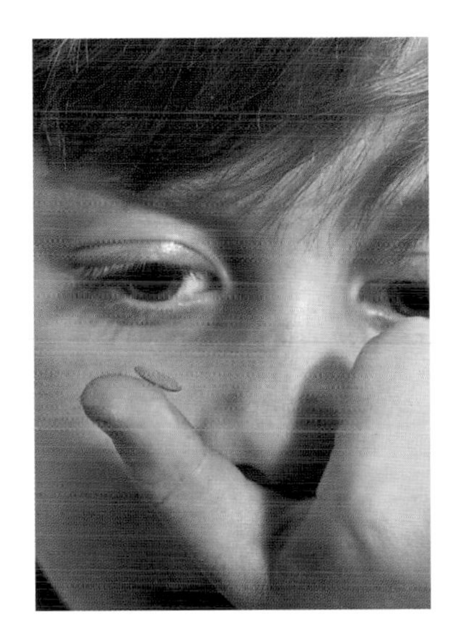

Some people wear contact lenses instead of glasses. Contact lenses are made of clear plastic. They float over the irises on the tears that cover the eyes.

Speaking of Talking

Take a deep breath. Now let it out slowly and say "Ahhhhh." You will only be able to make this sound while there is air in your lungs. When you run out of air, there will be no sound. This shows you how important your lungs are for talking.

Have you ever noticed the small bump on your neck beneath your chin? That's your voice box, or **larynx** (LAR ingks). Your larynx is like a box with two pieces of tissue stretched across it. The pieces of tissue are your vocal cords. When you talk or sing, air from your lungs is pushed through the opening between your vocal cords. This makes your vocal cords shake, or vibrate. When they vibrate, they make a sound.

By using muscles to change the size and shape of the spaces inside your mouth and throat, you can make all kinds of sounds. You can talk and sing. You can even bark like a dog.

TRY THIS! 1

See for yourself how the voice box works. With an adult's permission, blow up a balloon. Then pinch the neck closed, so no air escapes. Do you hear anything? You shouldn't. Now stretch the neck of the balloon to make a narrow slit. What do you hear? As the air escapes, it makes a squealing sound.

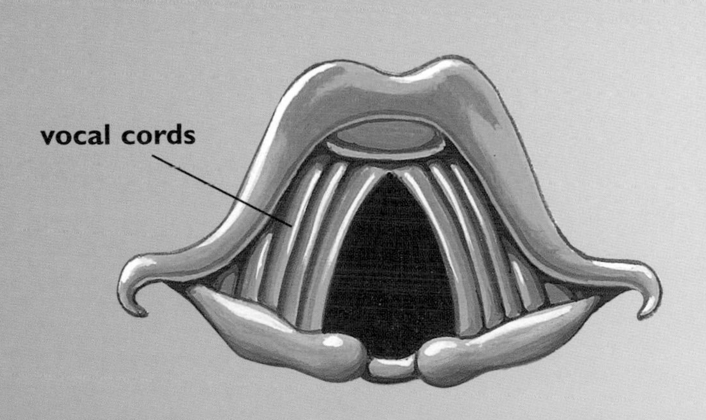

If you could see down the back of your throat, this is what your voice box would look like. You make noise by pushing air through the opening between your vocal cords. The sound you make depends on the size of this opening.

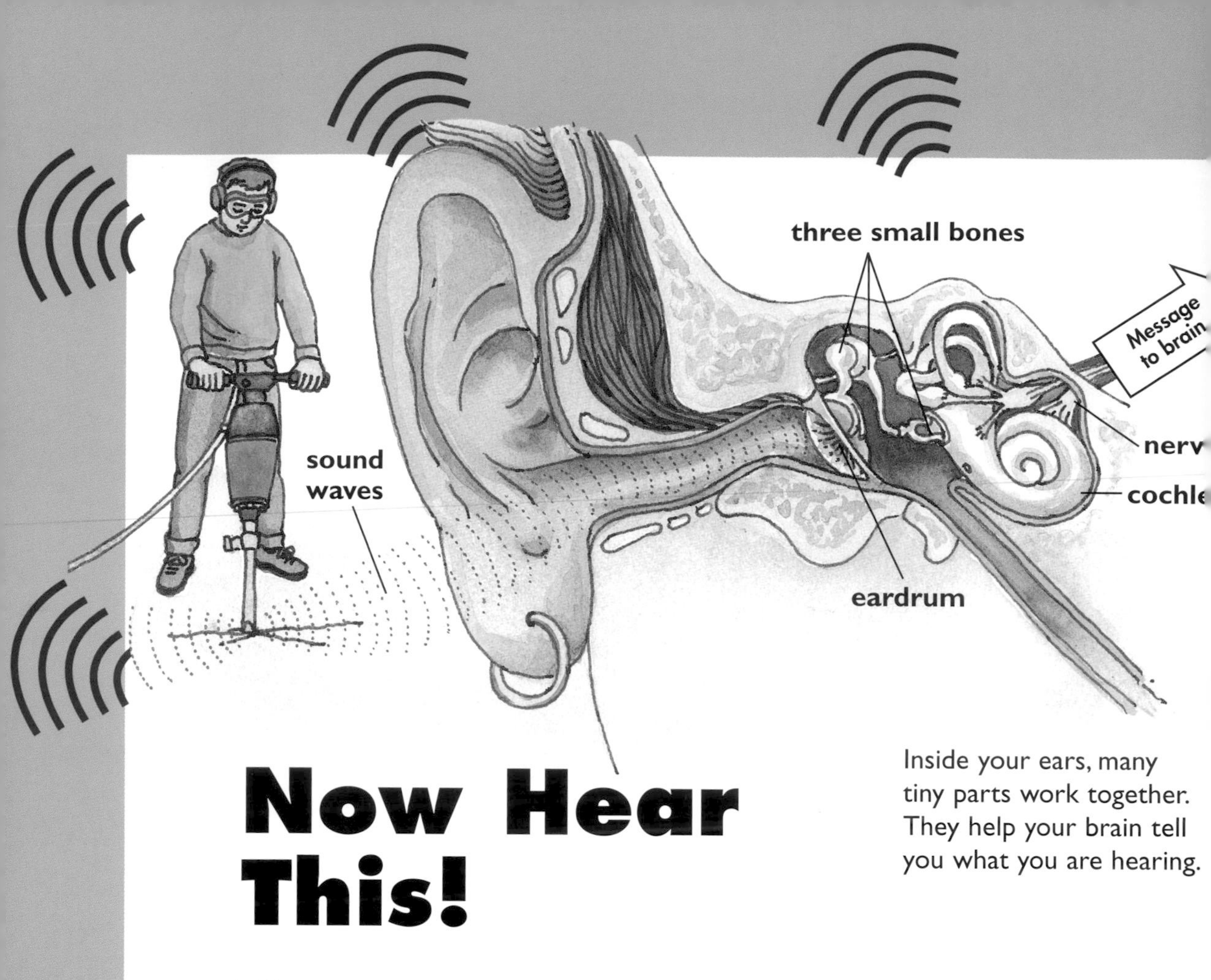

Inside your ears, many tiny parts work together. They help your brain tell you what you are hearing.

Now Hear This!

You hear things—people talking, car horns honking, and dogs barking. You know what these sounds are because your ears and brain work together.

When something makes a sound, the air around it moves, or vibrates. The vibrations travel through the air as sound waves. The sound waves enter your ear and bump against your eardrum. When the sound waves hit it, your eardrum moves.

When your eardrum moves, it bumps into three small bones. As each bone bumps the next, the third moves in and out of an opening in another part of the ear called the cochlea (KAHK lee uh). The cochlea looks like a shell.

Inside the cochlea are liquid and nerves. As the bone moves in and out of the cochlea, it makes waves in the liquid. The waves move across the nerves. The nerves carry messages to your brain. Your brain tells you what sound you are hearing.

TRY THIS! 1

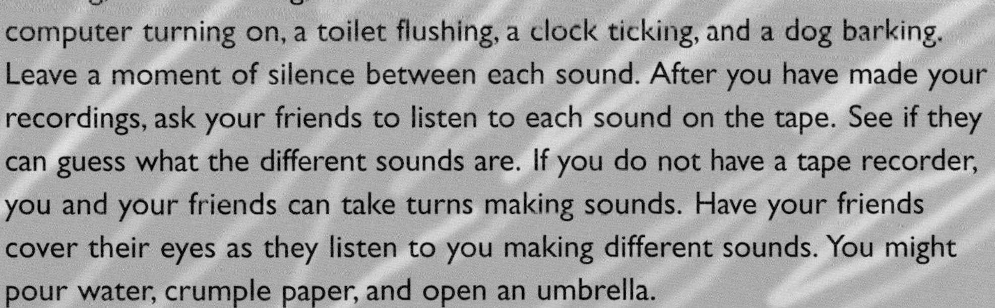

How well do you and your friends know the sounds around you? Make a tape recording of different sounds you hear every day, such as your parents' voices, a car starting, a door closing, a computer turning on, a toilet flushing, a clock ticking, and a dog barking. Leave a moment of silence between each sound. After you have made your recordings, ask your friends to listen to each sound on the tape. See if they can guess what the different sounds are. If you do not have a tape recorder, you and your friends can take turns making sounds. Have your friends cover their eyes as they listen to you making different sounds. You might pour water, crumple paper, and open an umbrella.

When Ears Need Help

A hearing aid is worn in the ear. It makes sounds louder.

In noisy places, you have to listen hard to hear things. You may put your hand to your ear to catch the sounds. Your ears are fine, yet sometimes you use your hands to help them.

Some people's ears need help all the time. These people are hard of hearing. Some other people cannot hear at all. They are deaf.

People who are hard of hearing may wear a hearing aid. A hearing aid makes sounds louder. It may allow people who are hard of hearing to use a telephone or hear more clearly the things people say. But hearing aids cannot help people who are completely deaf.

This boy is hard of hearing. He is learning how to speak more clearly with the help of a computer.

Deaf children and children who are severely hard of hearing have tremendous difficulty learning to speak. Normally, children learn to speak by listening to others. But deaf children cannot hear. Many people who are hard of hearing use speech-reading, finger spelling, or sign language to "talk" with other people. When they speech-read, they watch the speaker's mouth to see what the person is saying. This is also called lip-reading. With finger spelling, hand signals stand for each letter of the alphabet. In sign language, hand signals stand for words. Some people who are hard of hearing can learn to speak. They use little or no sign language. Instead they speak and speech-read to talk with others.

These people are using sign language to "talk."

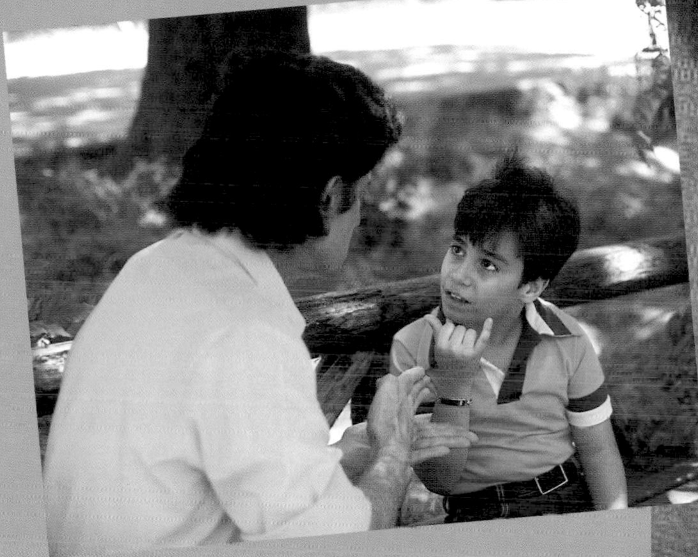

Try spelling *friend* to a friend!

Know Your Nose

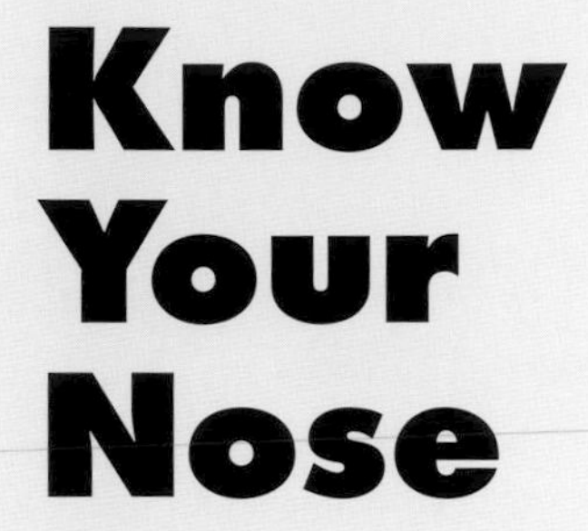

You're walking with your family when you smell something awful. Suddenly, everyone is looking at their shoes. It's your sister. She's stepped in the stuff a dog left behind.

The world is filled with smells—good ones and bad ones. With every breath you take, your nose tells you something about the air around you.

Imagine your dad is barbecuing chicken. You know this because you can smell it. You can smell the chicken because tiny bits or chemicals from it are floating around in the

air. These bits are much too small for your eyes to see, but your nose picks them up. They float into your nose through your nostrils. They enter your nostrils with the air you breathe.

After entering your nostrils, the air, with the tiny bits of chicken in it, moves up into a space at the top of your nose. This space is covered with nerves. The nerves receive the bits of chicken and send a message to your brain. Your brain tells you that chicken is cooking.

But you'll have to ask your dad when it'll be ready!

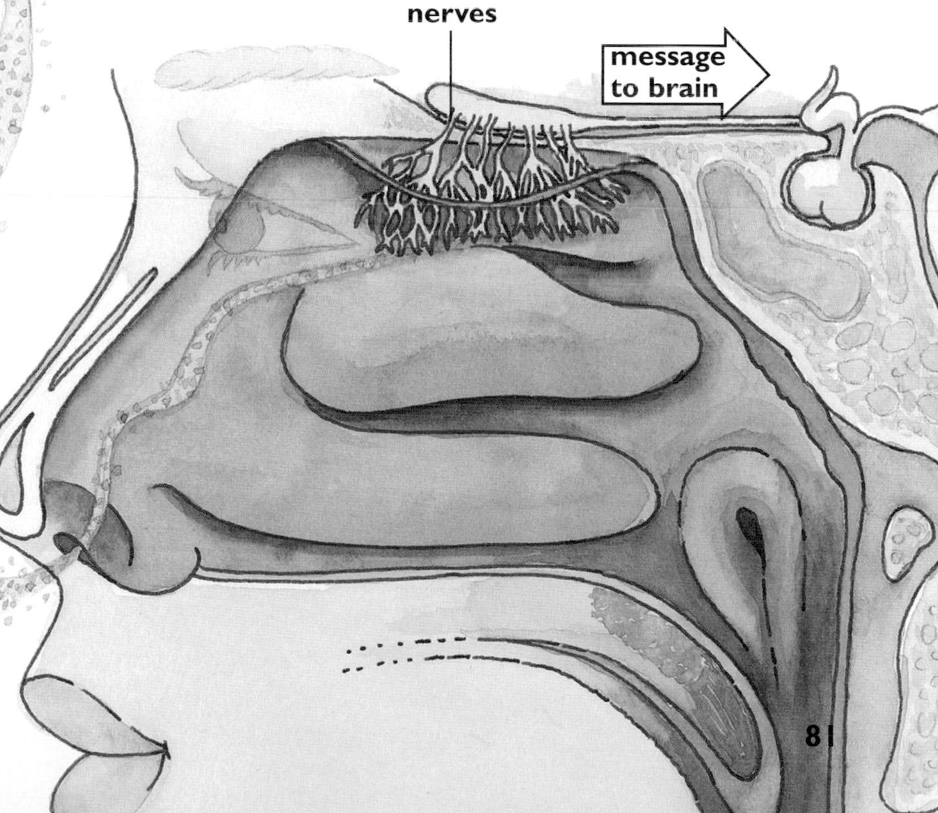

Smells travel into your nose and reach your nerves. The nerves send messages to your brain. Your brain tells you what the smells are.

A Matter of Taste

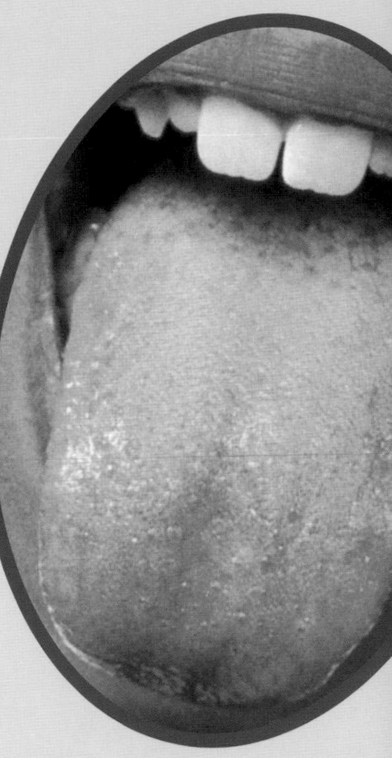

The bumps on your tongue contain groups of taste buds.

Think of your most favorite food. Is it cheese? Is it peanut butter? Or is it chocolate ice cream with hot fudge? Now think of a food you can't stand to eat. Do you just dread those days that you find it on your plate?

You know what you like to eat—and what you don't like—because you can taste your food as it tumbles over your tongue.

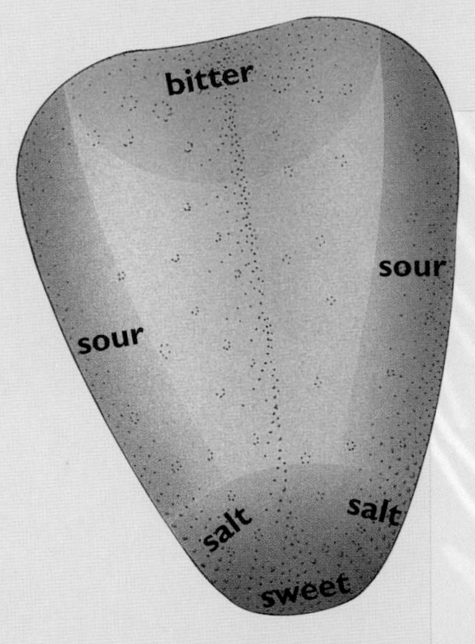

KNOW It All!

Different taste buds are experts in different tastes! That is why you may taste sweets best on the front and center of your tongue. You taste salty food at the front left and right sides, and you taste sour foods farther back along the sides. The taste buds for bitter foods are at the back of the tongue.

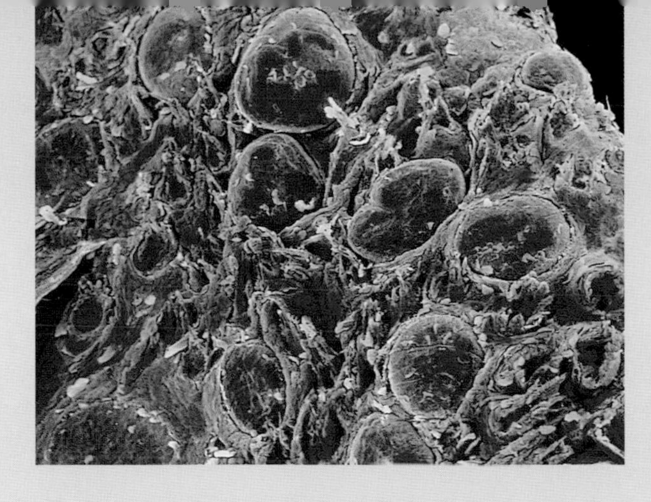

This is what taste buds look like through a microscope.

The front, back, and edges of your tongue are covered with little bumps. Take a look at your tongue and you'll see them. These bumps have groups of taste buds. Each taste bud has tiny nerves that send messages to your brain. Quick as a flash, your brain tells you what you are tasting.

Your sense of smell has a lot to do with how you taste things too. Think about the last time you had a cold. Do you remember trying to eat? You probably could not taste your food very well. That's because you can't smell what you are eating when your nose is stuffed up.

Test Yourself!

How well do you know your tastes and smells? Try these tests and find out. You need two or more people. One person is the tester. The others are the players.

You Will Need:

a blindfold for each player
spoons or forks for each player
foods with different flavors, such as a lemon, salty crackers, butter, vinegar, raw apple, raw potato, onion, jelly, honey, pudding

What To Do For Taste Tests:

1. Prepare a number of testers by placing different foods in bowls or plates. Don't let the players see them.

2. Have each player put on a blindfold. Ask the players to pinch their noses and take a small taste of a food.

3. After every player has tasted the food, ask each one to name the taste. If no one can name it, let the players try it without pinching their noses.

4. Repeat with the different foods. Take turns being the tester.

Which foods were easiest to name? Which ones were more difficult?

What To Do For Smell Tests:

1. Prepare a number of different "smell" jars by placing a small bit of each food or spice in each jar. Don't let the players see them.

2. Have each player put on a blindfold. Open a jar and allow each player to smell it pretty closely.

3. After every player has smelled the jar, ask each one to name the smell.

4. Repeat with the different smell jars. Take turns being the tester.

After the players have smelled all the jars, ask them which smells were easiest to name.

You Will Need:

a blindfold for each player
10 small jars with lids
10 different foods or spices that have strong odors, such as vanilla, peanut butter, onion, sage, cinnamon, and peppermint

A Touchy Subject

Everything has a "feel" to it. You know how things feel because you have nerves over every inch of your body. When something touches you, even lightly, it presses one or more nerves in your skin. The nerves carry a message to your brain, and your brain tells you how the thing feels.

Each nerve in your skin has a certain job. You have nerves for pressure, heat, cold, and pain. If you scrape your leg, the nerves for pain tell your brain, "That hurts!"

Nerves in your skin allow you to feel things.

Some parts of your body are more sensitive to touch than others. For example, your tongue and fingertips are very sensitive. In your more sensitive areas, nerves are

closer together than they are in less sensitive parts. The nerves in your fingers are very close together. That is why your fingers are so good at feeling things.

TRY THIS! 1

Your back is not as sensitive as your fingertips. That's because the nerves in your back are farther apart than the nerves in your fingers. See for yourself. Ask a friend to touch your back with two unsharpened pencils at the same time, first close together and then farther apart. It will feel as if your friend is using only one pencil until the two pencils are quite far apart.

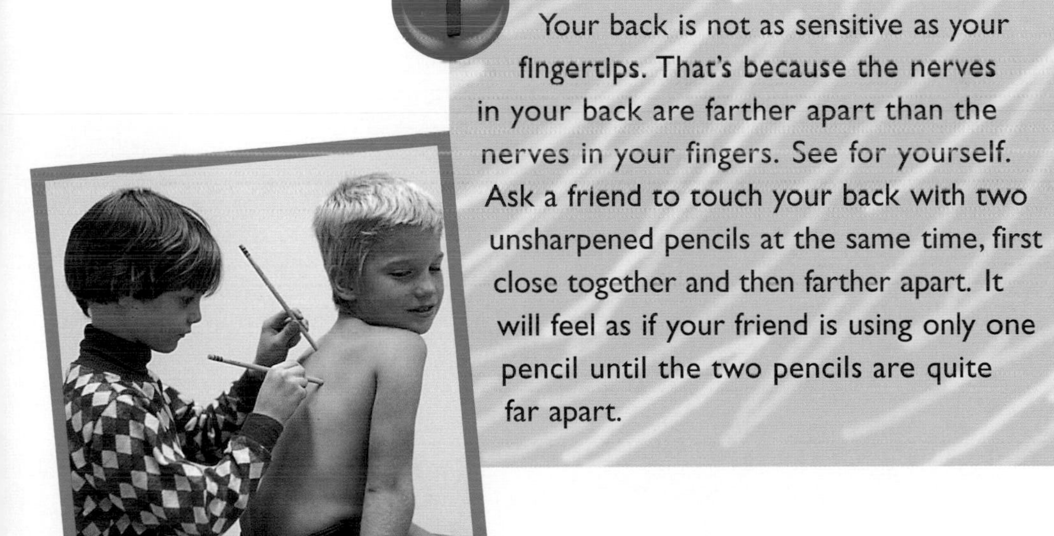

Things You Don't See

Take a close look at this picture. All the friends can see one another as well as the campfire and the trees. But they are using their other senses too. How many things can they hear? Name them. Can you find some things they can smell? What things can they feel? Find as many as you can. Some answers are printed at the bottom of the next page.

Possible Answers: **Hear**—owl hooting, wolf howling, boy calling, leaves rustling, fire crackling, friends singing, waves lapping; **smell**—smoke, hot dog cooking, skunk odor; **feel**—bandage on knee, heat from fire, thorn in foot, wind, dog's paws.

Growing and Changing

Today you are a child. One day, you will be a grown-up. As you grow to become an adult, you will not notice how you change from day to day. But you will notice the changes over years, months, or sometimes even weeks.

Sometimes, you will notice when you try on clothes or shoes. Things that used to fit you may seem too small. You may also notice when you measure or weigh yourself. Over time, you will see that you have grown taller or heavier.

You especially will notice how you have grown when you look at old pictures of yourself. You will see that changes have taken place in your face and your body. You will look bigger, stronger, and older than you once did.

Before You Were Born

Before you were born, you were warm and safe inside your mother's body. How did you get there?

Inside your mother was a special kind of cell called an egg. It was smaller than a grain of sand, smaller than the tiniest dot you can make with your pencil.

Inside your father was another special cell called a sperm. It was even smaller than the egg, and it looked a bit like a tadpole.

To make you, the sperm cell and the egg cell came together inside your mother's body. They joined and became one cell. When that happened, a new life began—your life.

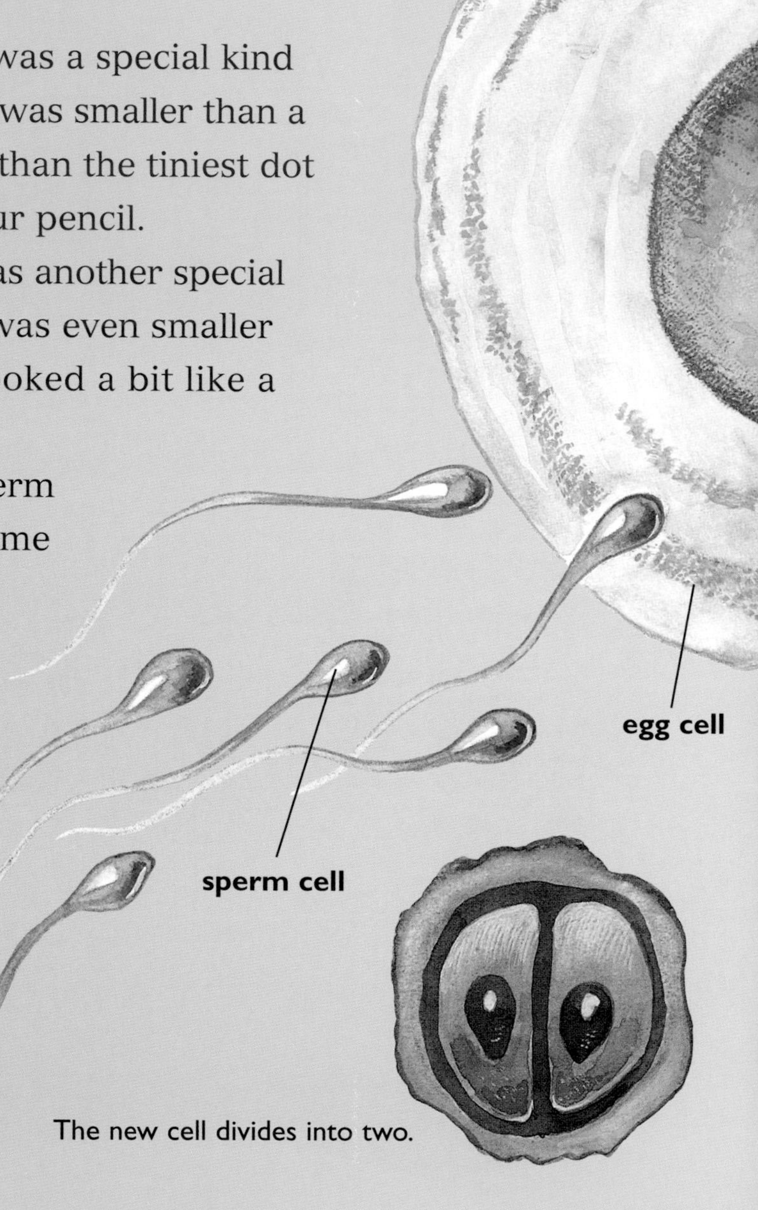

The new cell divides into two.

Soon that cell began to divide. It divided into two cells. The two cells divided into four. The four cells divided into eight. The tiny cells stayed together and continued to divide.

At first, all the cells seemed to be alike. Then, each cell began to do its own job. Some cells became skin cells. Others became bone cells or nerve cells or brain cells.

This is how you grew before you were born.

A sperm cell and an egg cell come together to make a new life.

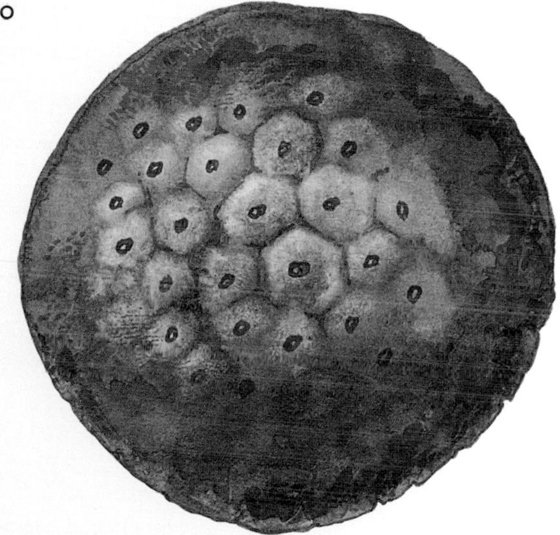

The dividing goes on and on. The cells will form a tiny baby.

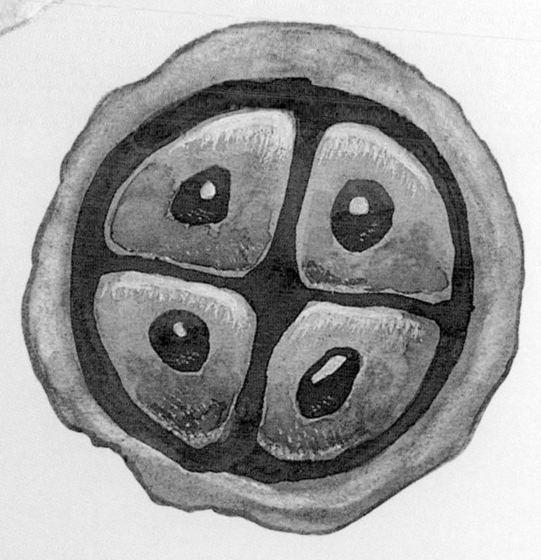

The two cells divide into four.

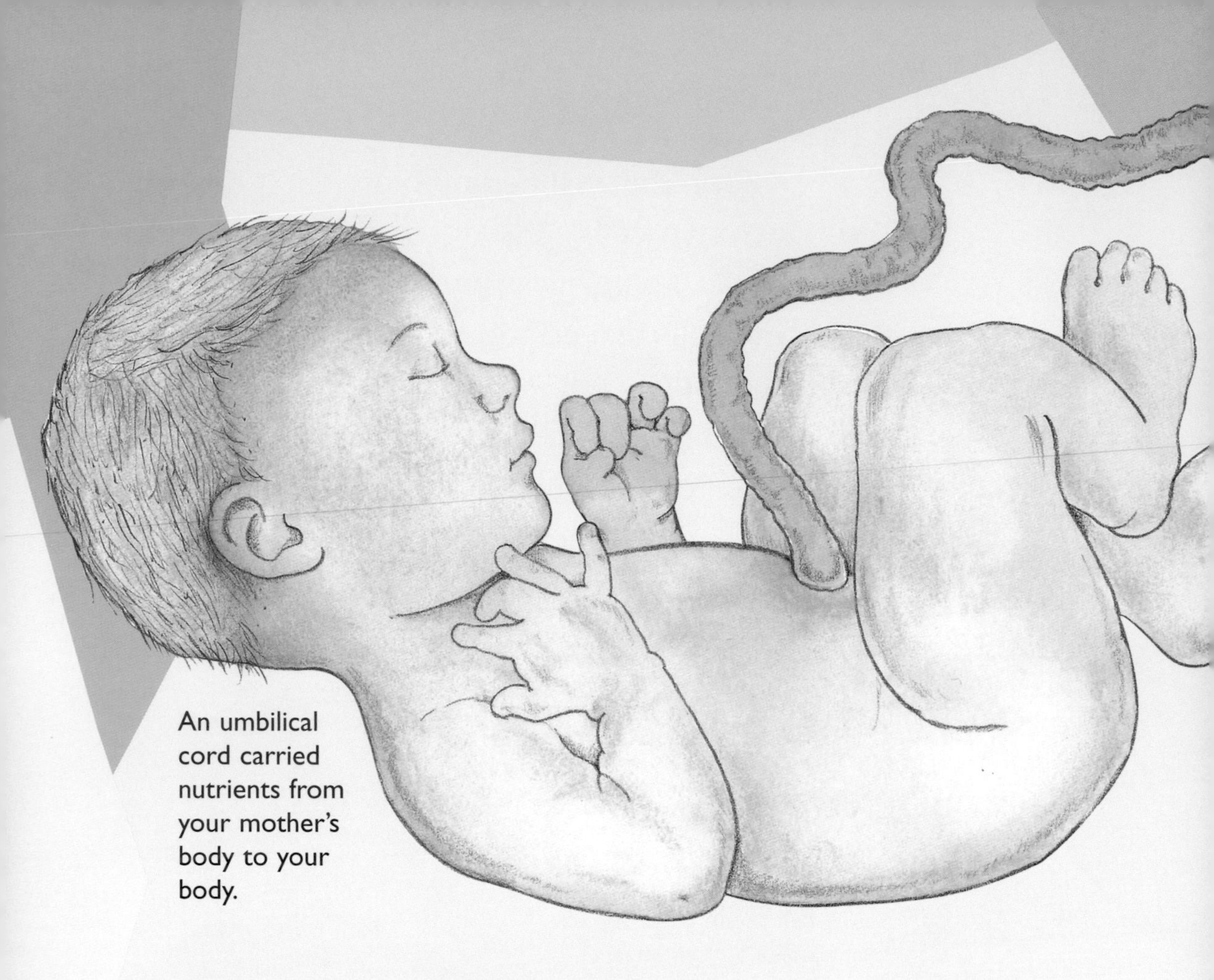

An umbilical cord carried nutrients from your mother's body to your body.

Waiting to Be Born

You had a lot of growing to do before you were ready to be born. The egg and the sperm that had joined together needed a safe, warm place in which to grow. That place was inside your mother's body.

As you grew, parts of your mother's body became larger to make room for you. You were safe and warm there, and you were fed through a cord called an **umbilical cord** (uhm BIHL uh kuhl kawrd). The cord joined you to your mother. Blood flowed through the umbilical cord. The blood carried nutrients from your mother's body to your body. The place where this cord was attached to your body is now your navel, or bellybutton.

As you grew, you began to move around. You moved your arms. You kicked your legs. Your mother could feel you moving and growing larger. For about nine months, you grew and changed shape. Then you were ready to come into the world.

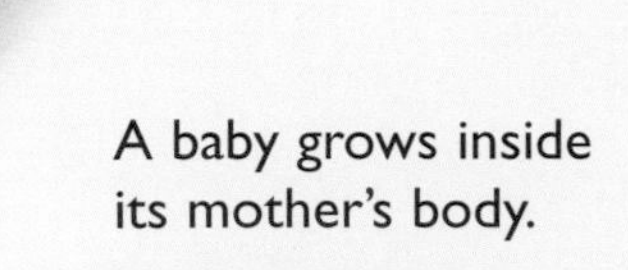

A baby grows inside its mother's body.

Being Born

When you were ready to be born, your mother felt some aches around her belly. She knew what the aches meant. You were ready to be born! Her muscles were working to push you out.

The muscles kept working until, finally, your mother felt a pushing. The pushing got quicker and stronger. At last you probably were pushed out of her body—head first—through her vagina.

After you were born, your mother held you close. The cord that joined you to your mother was cut, because you did not need it anymore.

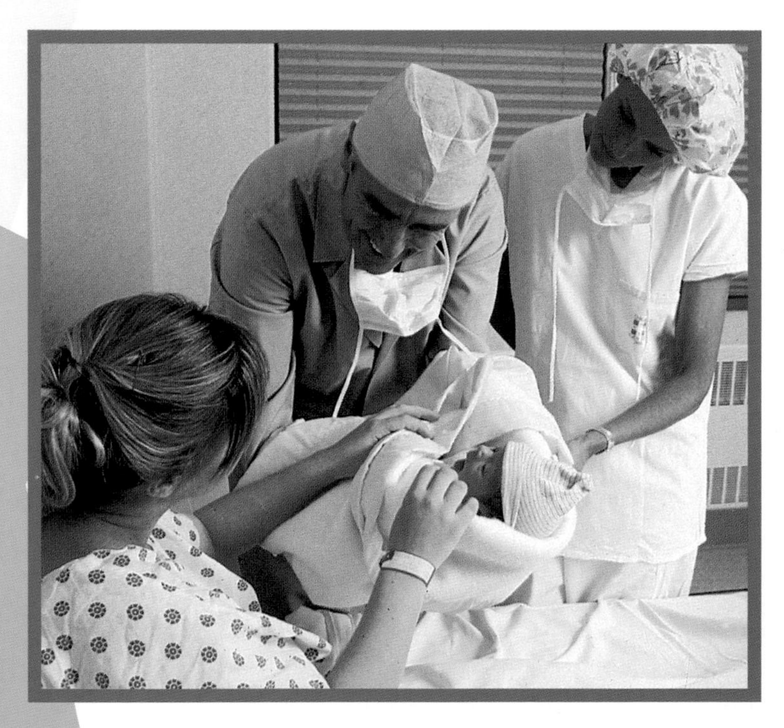

The doctors and nurses clean and dress the new baby. Then they return the baby to the mother.

After a short visit with your mother, lots of new things may have happened to you. Nurses check newborn babies to make sure they are healthy. They weigh, measure, bathe, and dress new babies too. Most babies weigh about 7 1/2 pounds (3.4 kilograms) when they are born. In a hospital, nurses put name tags on newborn babies' wrists and ankles and put their fingerprints and footprints on paper.

When you were all checked over, you were handed back to your family.

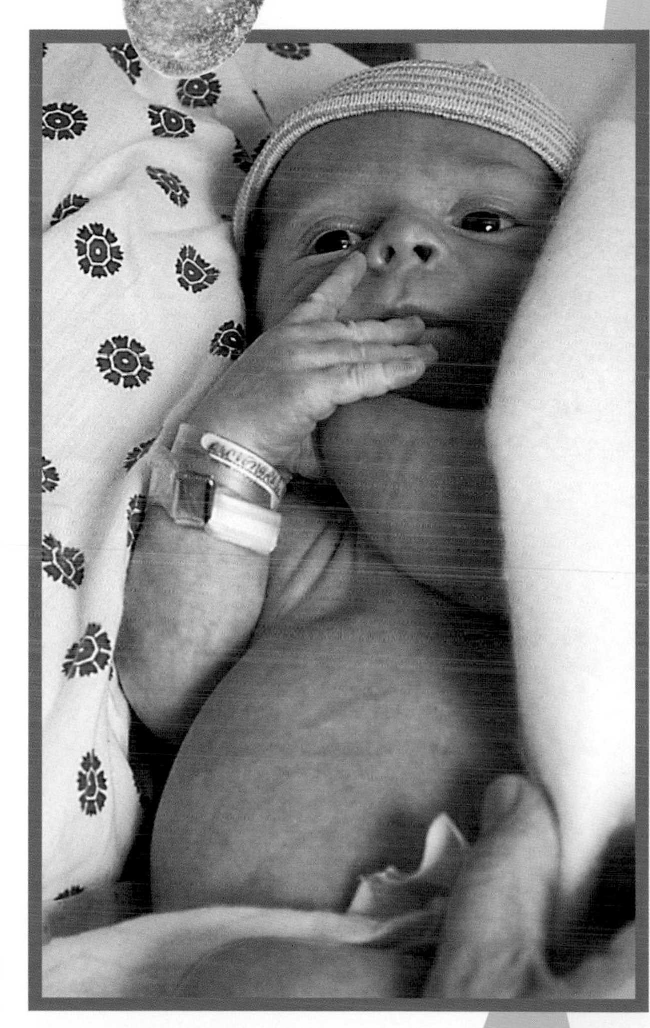

A healthy new baby is safe in mother's arms.

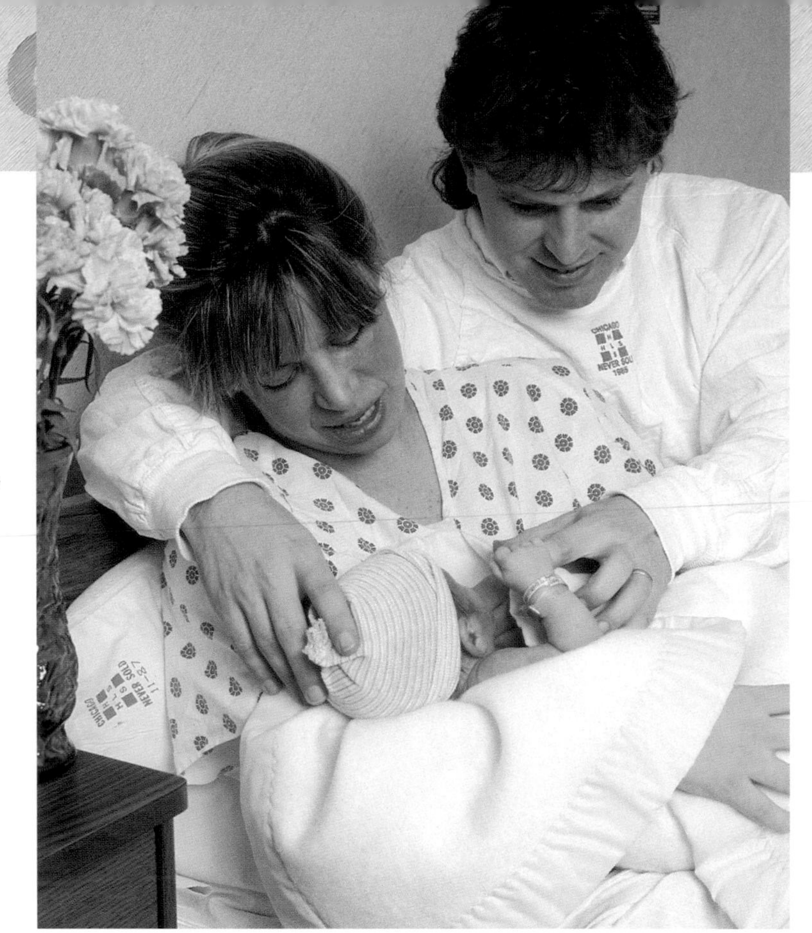

Mom and Dad meet their new baby.

The New You

A baby is called a newborn for about a month after birth. A newborn baby spends most of the time sleeping. The head makes up about one-fourth of a newborn's body. Look at baby pictures of people in your family. Can you tell how big a baby's head is compared to the rest of the body?

Most things newborn babies do just happen. They do not need to think about doing them. They can suck, swallow, move their arms and legs, and cry. But they cannot sit up, crawl, or walk yet. Newborn babies can't even hold their heads up. Their neck muscles are not strong enough.

Newborn babies can tell when it is dark or light, and they can see things in front of them. They can also hear, and they quickly learn to recognize their parent's voice.

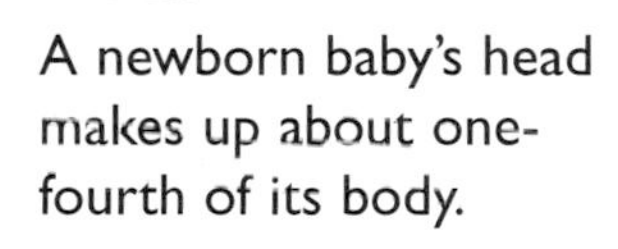

A newborn baby's head makes up about one-fourth of its body.

During the first year of life, babies change in many ways. They learn to hold up their heads. They learn to roll over, sit, crawl, and stand. Their bodies become much bigger and stronger.

If you have baby pictures of yourself, take a look at them. How have you changed?

KNOW It All!

Crying is the beginning of language for a person. It is the only way newborn babies can tell people how they feel. They cry to let people know they are hungry, tired, or need a diaper change.

Who Will You Look Like?

Have you ever noticed how members of a family look alike? Do your friends look like their parents? Do you look like anyone in particular?

Parents pass along many things to their children when their eggs and sperm cells come together. The eggs contain tiny things called **genes** (jeenz). The sperm cells contain genes too. Each gene is like an order. Some genes are an order for height. Others are an order for hair color. There are thousands of these orders. All together they tell a body how to grow into a special, one-of-a-kind person.

The things people do every day also make them who they are. For example, the things people eat have something to do with how tall or how big their bodies will be.

So what about you? Who will you look like? Some of your genes came from your father, so you will look a little like him. Some genes came from your mother, so you will look a little like her. Your parents got their genes from their parents, so you will look a little like your grandparents too. Mostly, you will look exactly like YOU.

KNOW It All! Have you ever seen a pair of sisters or brothers who look exactly alike? Two sisters or two brothers who look exactly alike are called identical twins. But not all twins look alike. Twins that don't are called fraternal (fruh TUHR nuhl) twins.

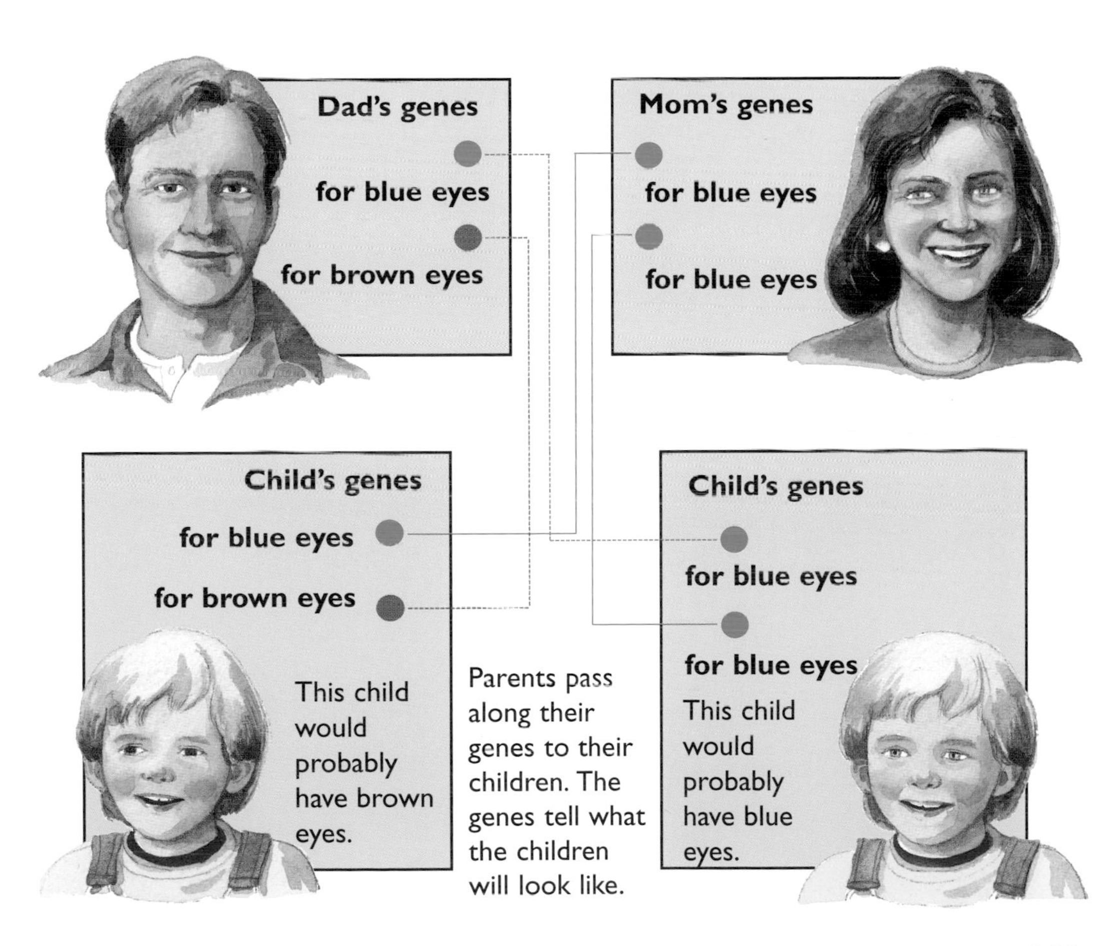

Parents pass along their genes to their children. The genes tell what the children will look like.

Your Growing Bones

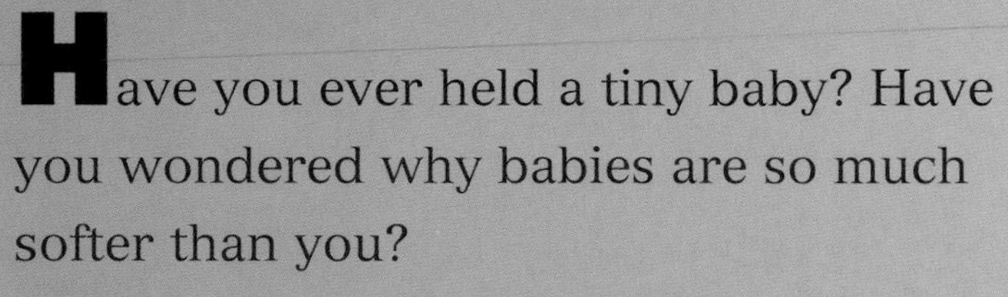

Have you ever held a tiny baby? Have you wondered why babies are so much softer than you?

One reason babies are softer is that their bones have not hardened yet. When they are born, babies have more bones than an adult and a lot of cartilage. But, their bone cells work all the time to become bigger and harder. Some even grow together. In fact, as babies grow, most of their cartilage turns into bone, except for parts of the nose, ears, and ribs. Fully grown adults have about 206 bones.

When doctors want to check how a child's bones are growing, they may take X rays of the wrists. Some children's wrist bones grow quickly. Others grow more slowly. The important thing is that the bones are growing in a healthy way. If your wrist bones look healthy on an X ray, then all the other bones in your body are probably growing the way they should, too.

When your bones grow, your body grows too.

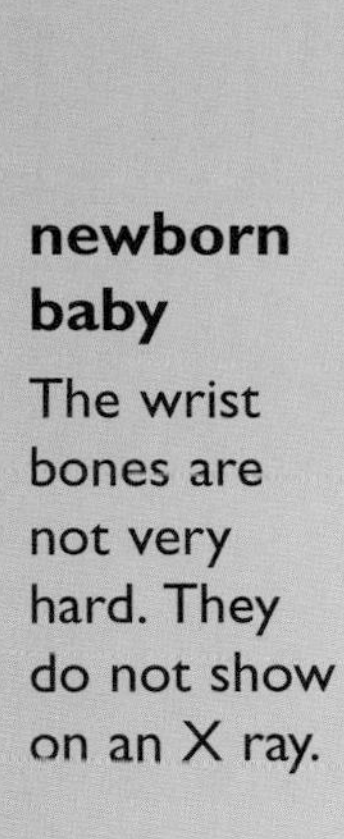

newborn baby

The wrist bones are not very hard. They do not show on an X ray.

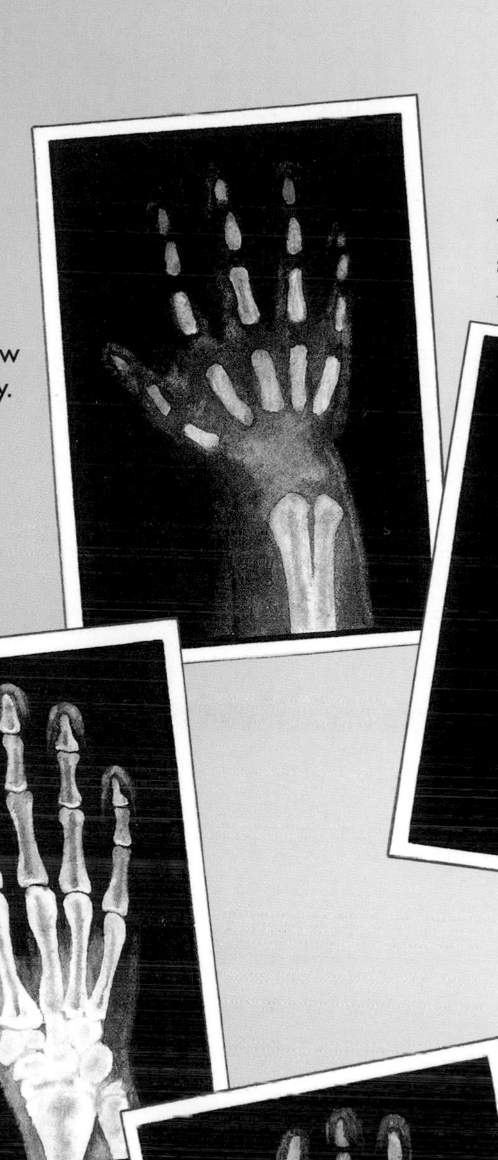

1-year-old

Two small, round bones are the first wrist bones to show on an X ray.

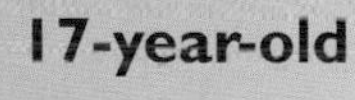

17-year-old

This X ray shows that all eight wrist bones have grown.

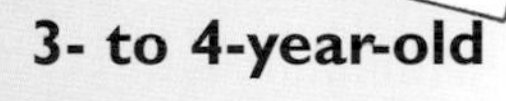

3- to 4-year-old

This X ray shows four wrist bones.

7-year-old

This X ray shows six wrist bones.

How Tall Will You Be?

You are always growing. It is the easiest thing you do. It just happens. You cannot see yourself grow. You may not seem to be much taller today than you were last year, but the clothes you wore last year are too small for you now. So you know you have grown.

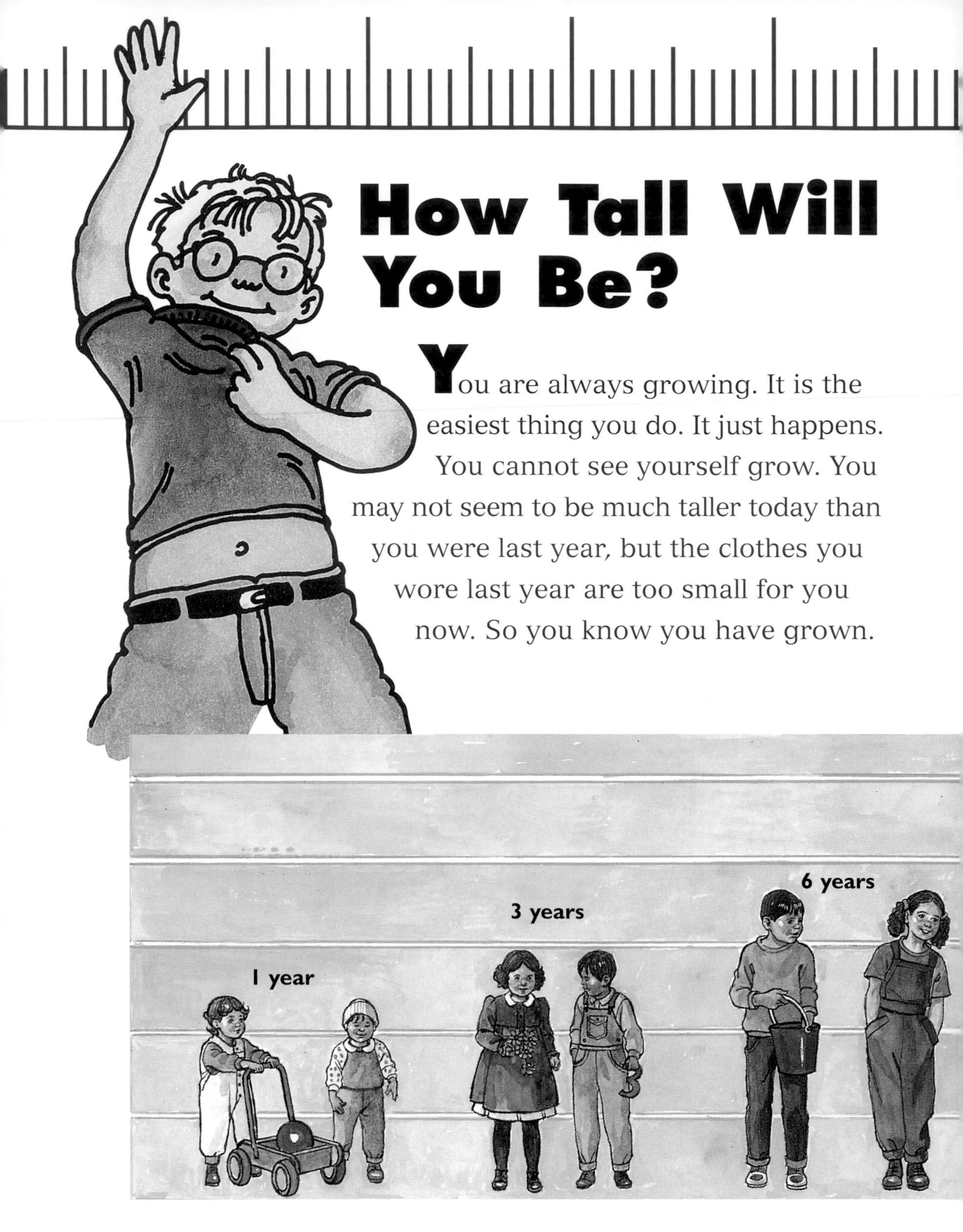

KNOW It All!

Place a growth chart on a wall somewhere in your home. On each birthday, mark your height on the chart. As the years go by, you will be able to see how much you have grown.

How does your body grow?

Each day the cells in your body grow and divide. Each day your muscles have more cells in them. Your bones have more cells in them too. So each day they grow a little bigger.

By the time you are in your late teens, your legs will be about five times as long as they were when you were a baby. Your arms will be about four times as long. Your head will be about twice as big.

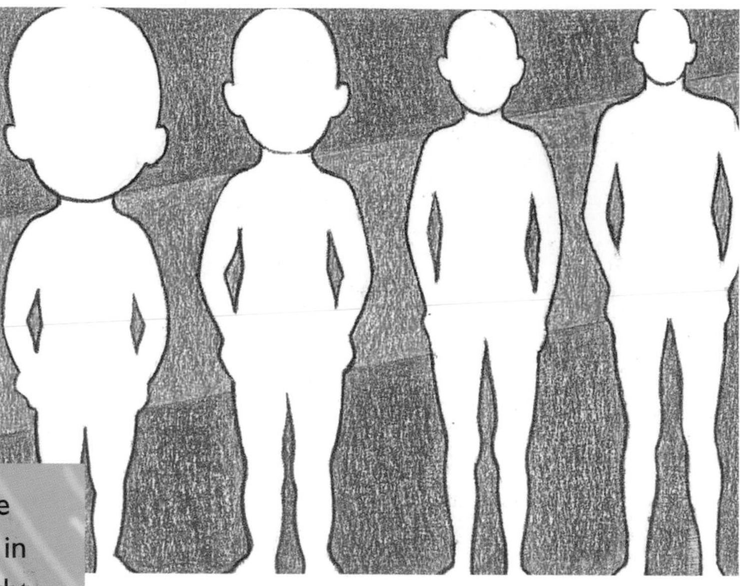

KNOW It All!

Babies are measured in length, not height. This is because they can't stand up to be measured. When you were born, your head made up about one-fourth of your body's length. By the time you finish growing, it will only make up about one-eighth of your height.

You may wonder why you do not keep on growing and never stop. One reason is that while your body makes new cells, other cells wear out. But a more important reason has to do with tiny organs called glands. Glands make special chemicals that your body uses.

You have two kinds of glands. Some glands make liquids such as sweat, tears, and saliva. Other glands make chemicals called **hormones** (HAWR mohnz) and put them into your blood. In your blood, hormones make things happen.

The **pituitary** (pih TOO uh TEHR ee) gland puts growth hormone into your blood. The blood carries it to the body parts that need to grow.

Babies grow very fast because their bodies make new cells a lot faster than the others wear out. You grew most rapidly during your first two years of life. Your growth will be slower until you are about 12. Then your body will start to grow rapidly again. Some people call this a "growth spurt."

Before the growth spurt begins, boys and girls are almost the same height. Girls begin their growth spurt earlier than boys, but boys usually grow more. So they tend to be taller when the growth spurt ends.

One day, your glands will tell your body to stop growing. Then you will not grow any taller.

TRY THIS! 1

When someone measures you, stand straight against a wall and have a helper mark a line at the top of your head. Unless you stand against a growth chart, use a tape measurer to measure from the floor to the line your helper marks. At least once each year, have your growth measured. Then write down your height, the date, and your age. It's fun to see how much you have grown from year to year or more often.

Families

Everywhere you look, families are different. Some children live with their birth parents, who are the mother and father to whom they were born. Some children are adopted. Their mother and father chose them to be part of their family.

Some families are just parents and children.

Other children live with their mother and stepfather. Or maybe they live with their father and stepmother. In many such families, brothers and sisters from one family live with brothers and sisters from another family.

Many children live with just their mother or just their father. Other children live with their grandmother or grandfather, or with both grandparents.

And still others live with another relative, such as an aunt or uncle.

No matter what kind of family you have and no matter who you live with, you are part of a family. And all families work in the same way. The people in a family do a lot for each other. They stick up for one another. They are happy, sad, and angry with one another. They work and play together. They share things and responsibilities.

What is your family like?

Some children live with their grandparents.

Some children have large families that include aunts, uncles, and grandparents.

Eric
Sara
Jared
Annika
Dad
Mom
Grandma & Grandpa
Grandpa & Grandma
Our Family Tree

Families

The people who live with you are your family. There are other people who are part of your family also, but they may not live with you. They are your relatives.

Some families have many brothers and sisters. Other families have only one or two. Still other families have no brothers or sisters at all.

All families have grandparents. One of your grandmas is your father's mother, and one of your grandmas is your mother's mother. One of your grandpas is your mother's father, and one of your grandpas is your father's father.

You may have aunts and uncles, too. Some aunts are your mother's sisters, and some are your father's sisters. Some uncles are your father's brothers, and some are your mother's brothers.

Your aunts and uncles may have husbands and wives. They are your uncles and aunts too. Some of your aunts and uncles may have children. These children are your cousins.

All families are different. Who's in your family? Who are your relatives?

Your Family News

Whether your family is large or small, there is always something new to tell each other.

A newspaper is one way that people find out about things. You can get all kinds of important information from them. Make a family newspaper and share the news!

You Will Need:

big sheets of plain paper (or small ones taped together)

colored pencils

copies or scans of photographs or drawings of people in your family

What To Do:

1. Think of a name for your family newspaper. What will you call it? For example, The Dalton Daily, The Taylor Times, The Paxton Paper, The Nixon News, or The Redding Reader. Ask an adult to help you write the name across the top of the front page of your newspaper. Use big letters.

2. Next, add news stories. What has happened to people in your family? Maybe a relative had a baby, someone graduated from school, or someone moved. You can write the stories yourself or ask someone to help you. You can also ask people in your family to write stories, and you can paste them on the paper. Try to include news about everyone—including stepbrothers, stepsisters, grandparents, aunts, uncles, and cousins. Don't forget to give your stories headlines, or titles.

3. Add pictures to some of the stories. You can draw pictures with crayons or markers. You can also paste on copies and printouts of pictures.

Share your newspaper with your family when you have finished. If any of your relatives live far away, you could send them a copy of your newspaper. They will be happy to hear the news!

Thoughts and Feelings

Along with things like bones and blood, inside you are thoughts and feelings. They cannot be seen or touched, but they are also very important in making you the special person that you are.

No one can know you as well as you know yourself. Only you know all your thoughts, your feelings, and your dreams.

When you were very small, you saw the world from your parents' arms.

Your Growing World

At first your world was small. It was only as big as your parents' arms. You quickly learned to recognize your mother's and father's faces. You liked to be close to them.

Soon your world grew bigger. Your home and all the things in it were part of your world. You learned to crawl, so you moved around and explored your growing world.

As you grew bigger, your world grew bigger too. Your parents took you to new places—parks, stores, restaurants, and places to play. You watched and listened to learn more about these places. You met new people. You met other people in your family, your parents' friends, other children, and babysitters.

As you grow older, your world continues to grow. It grows to include your school, your friends' homes, playing fields, and swimming pools. Every time you go some place new, you will add to your ever-growing world.

As you grow bigger, your world grows bigger too.

TRY THIS! 2

Think of all the different places you have been today—for example, school, the mall, the doctor's office, and home. Ask an adult to help you make a list of these places. Now draw a picture of each place. Have an adult help you write a sentence or two about your drawings. Next time, think of all the places you have been in a week.

Feeling at Home in School

School is a place where you learn more about your world and make new friends.

The first time you went to school, you did not know what to expect. There were so many new faces. You may have been a little scared. Soon you learned things and made friends.

The first day of any new school year is sometimes like that very first day. It's exciting. You wake up early in the morning. You eat breakfast quickly. You gather up your new school supplies. You do not want to be late.

Lots of questions race through your mind. What will your new teacher and classroom be like? Where will you sit? What new things will you learn?

Maybe you have not seen your school friends all summer. There will be a lot to talk about. There might be new children in the classroom—new friends. Maybe you will be the new child in the classroom. If so, you might be a little scared or shy. Will the other children like the things you like? What if you get lost in the school? These are normal feelings.

A new school year is always a little strange at first. Soon everything will become friendly and familiar. In time, you will feel right at home.

Learning About the World

As you grow, you think and wonder. You think of questions, and you try to find the answers. You might wonder why it does not hurt to cut your hair. Why do you yawn? What, exactly, do your fingerprints look like?

You search for the answers to these questions by using your eyes, reading

Have you ever wondered why it doesn't hurt to cut your hair?

books, using the computer, or asking people. Believe it or not, when you do this searching, you are doing what scientists do.

You find out from looking through a magnifying glass what your fingerprints look like. You find out from reading an encyclopedia that cutting your hair does not hurt because there are no nerves in your hair. You feel pain only where there are nerves. You find out from asking your dad that you yawn because you are tired. The gulps of air you take in as you yawn bring extra oxygen into your body and make you feel more awake.

Have you ever wondered why people yawn? Where would you go to find the answer?

Some things are fun to think about. Some are confusing. You might wonder why you were born. What does being alive mean, and why do people die? You might ask your parents, a teacher, or a friend. Try to find the answers together.

The more you learn, the more you will want to know!

Sometimes you feel angry at your brothers and sisters.

Your Ever-Changing Feelings

Have you ever noticed how quickly your feelings can change? One day you might feel happy because you made a new friend. The next day you might feel

sad because your friend seems to like someone else better.

Understanding how and why your feelings change is part of growing up. Sometimes feelings can be very confusing.

Not all feelings are good, but it is still okay to have them. It is also okay to let people know how you feel—and why you feel that way. But it is not okay to do whatever your feelings make you feel like doing. It is not okay to hit someone or call someone a name because you are angry.

How do you think this boy is feeling? How is he telling you how he feels?

You tell people how you are feeling in many ways. You tell them with your words, your face, and what you do with your body. When you are angry you might want to frown, make a fist, or yell. But you might find it more helpful to talk.

If your feelings upset you, talk to someone you trust. You will learn that everyone feels the same way you do, at some time or another.

Playing with your friends can make you happy.

Happy and Sad Face Puppets

Have fun sharing feelings with a friend. Get together with a friend. Then each of you make a puppet.

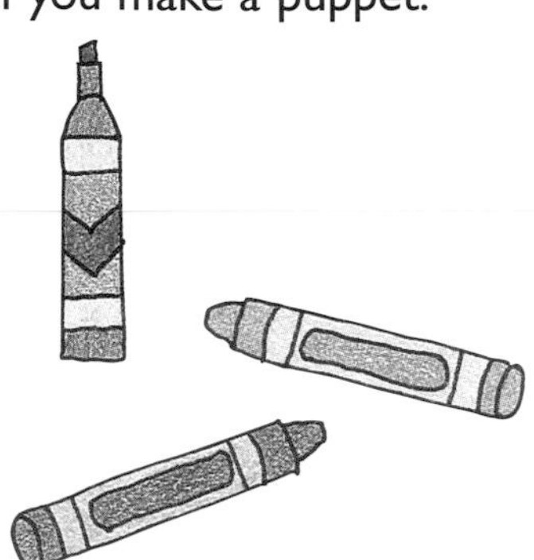

You Will Need:

4 paper plates
2 craft sticks
glue or tape
crayons or markers
construction paper and yarn, if desired

What To Do:

1. On the front of one plate, use crayons or markers to draw a happy face. On the front of another plate, draw a sad face. If you would like, glue yarn to the plates for hair. You can also add clothes and other decorations.

2. Glue or tape a craft stick to the back of one of the plates, as shown. This will be the handle for your puppet.

3. Glue the back sides of the two plates together.

4. With your friend, take turns saying things that make you happy or sad, such as, "going to the park" or "getting a shot." Then hold up the side of the plate that shows how that thing makes you feel. If you would like, have the puppets talk to each other about their feelings.

You can make many puppets with different feelings. Their faces can look angry, surprised, or scared.

Being Friends

Who shares your secrets? Who is the first to know when something good or bad happens to you? Your friends, that's who!

Many people have a best friend. You might have a lot of other friends, too. Friends are people you feel safe with. You can trust your friends.

Sometimes your friends make you mad. But usually you do not stay angry for long. You know that your friends do not mean to hurt you.

Think of all the things you like about your friends. All your friends have something special about them that you like. You might like one friend because he is fun to be with or because she is a good listener.

Remember that you are a friend too. You need to be a friend to have a friend. Friends treat others just as they want to be treated. Always be the friend you would like to have.

Friends share secrets (friends don't tell).

Friends share good times (and bad, as well).

Friends share things with one another.

That's because friends like each other.

Of all the happy things there are,

Friends are the very best, by far.

What's the best way to make friends? You can make friends by:

- smiling and being nice,
- sharing a toy or game,
- telling a funny story,
- helping someone,
- listening to people without interrupting,
- asking polite questions to get to know people,
- saying nice things to make a person feel good,
- joining a group activity.

What does it mean to be a good friend? You are a good friend if you:

- are fun to be with,
- share things,
- make your friends feel good,
- care about how your friends feel,
- enjoy doing some of the same things as your friends do,
- accept your friends for who they are.

Everybody Is Different

Think of people you know and see every day. They are all different. They look different than you, and some believe in different things. Some people probably cannot do all the things that you can do. Others can do things you cannot do.

No one in the world looks exactly like you, and no one can do exactly the same things. You might be great at math, while your friend struggles with it. Your friend might be a good baseball player, while you cannot hit a baseball. What's nice is that the two of you can help each other.

Nobody is good at everything, but everybody is good at something—even someone who has a body part that does not work properly. Moving around easily

People do things in different ways. Try doing something a new way.

Everybody is good at something.

or seeing and hearing clearly are only some of the things that people can do. A person who cannot do these things is still able to do many other things.

When you think about something you cannot do, remember that it is only one part of you. There are other things you *can* do. All these things help make you a unique person.

TRY THIS! 1

What special things can each person in your family do? Draw a picture of each family member. Below each picture, list a few of that person's skills or talents.

Squares Are Not Bad

Having friends who are different from you can make you a better person and be fun. Read this story by Violet Salazar to find out why this is true.

Here are the Squares. They live all by themselves in Square Town.

Here are the Circles. They live all by themselves in Circle Town.

Here are the Triangles. They live all by themselves in Triangle Town.

Here are the Rectangles. They live all by themselves in Rectangle Town.

The Squares do not like the Circles.

The Circles do not like the Triangles.

The Triangles do not like the Rectangles.

The Rectangles do not like the Squares.

They do not like anyone but themselves. They think the others are stupid and lazy and mean and bad! bad! bad!

The Squares say this: "If you want to be smart and beautiful and good, you must have four sides exactly the same. If you don't have four sides exactly the same, then you are stupid and ugly and bad! bad! bad!"

The Circles say this: "If you want to be smart and beautiful and good, you must be perfectly round. If you are not perfectly round, then you are stupid and ugly and bad! bad! bad!"

The Triangles say this: "If you want to be smart and beautiful and good, you must have only three sides. If you do not have three sides, then you are stupid and ugly and bad! bad! bad!"

The Rectangles say this: "If you want to be smart and beautiful and good, you must have two short sides exactly the same, and you must have two long sides exactly the same. If you don't have two short sides and two long sides, then you are stupid and ugly and bad! bad! bad!"

One beautiful summer day, the little Squares and little Circles and little Triangles and little Rectangles went outside to play. But NOT together.

While they were playing, a terrible thing happened. The little Circles were playing on top of a hill. Some of them slipped and went rolling down the hill. Faster and faster, they rolled to the very bottom of the hill where the little

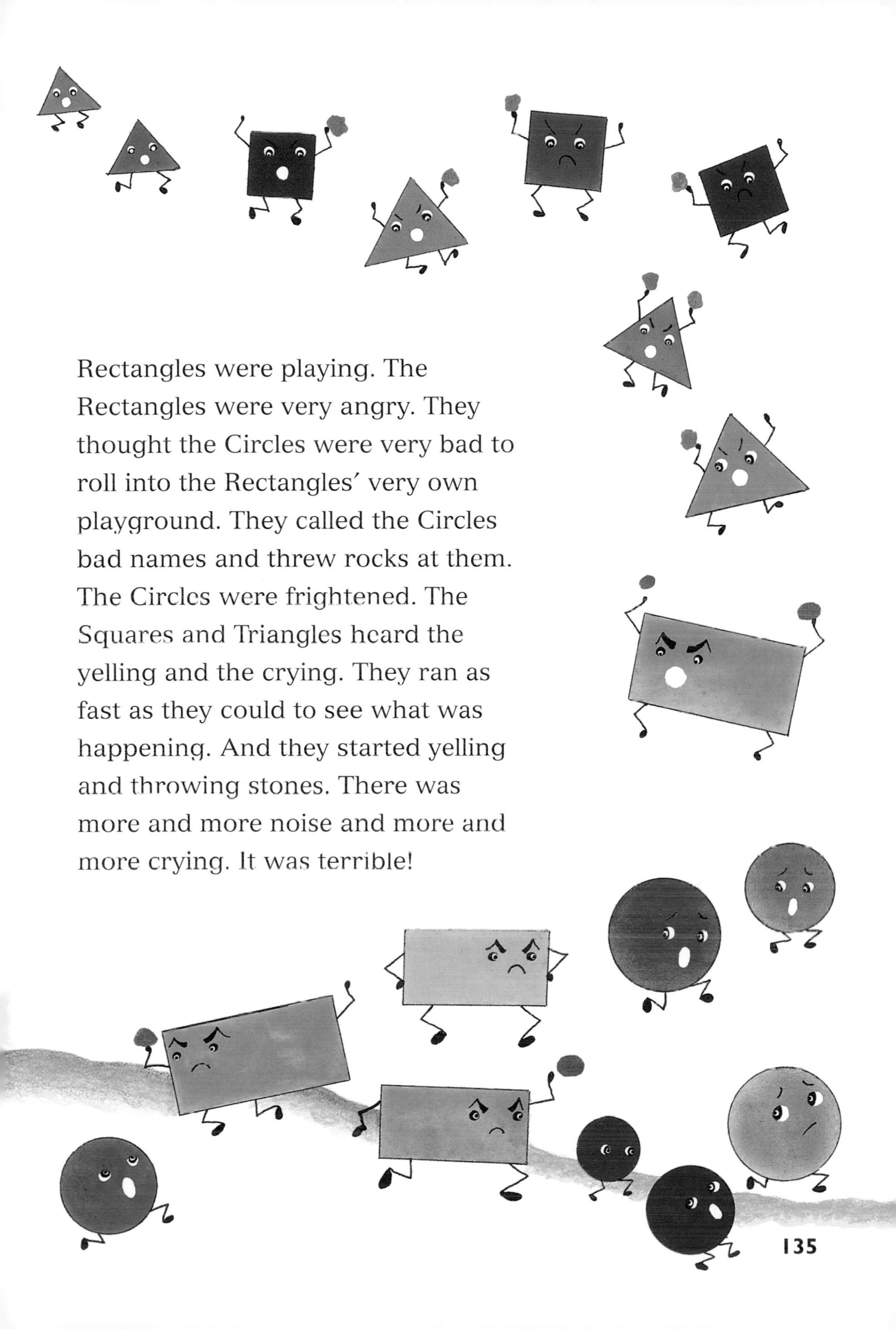

Rectangles were playing. The Rectangles were very angry. They thought the Circles were very bad to roll into the Rectangles' very own playground. They called the Circles bad names and threw rocks at them. The Circles were frightened. The Squares and Triangles heard the yelling and the crying. They ran as fast as they could to see what was happening. And they started yelling and throwing stones. There was more and more noise and more and more crying. It was terrible!

At last one of the Rectangles became so angry that he leaped into the air and came down right on top of the Circles.

Oh, wonder of wonders!

Everyone was absolutely quiet. No one said a word! They just looked and looked and LOOKED.

The Rectangle and Circles had made a wagon! A lovely, beautiful wagon!

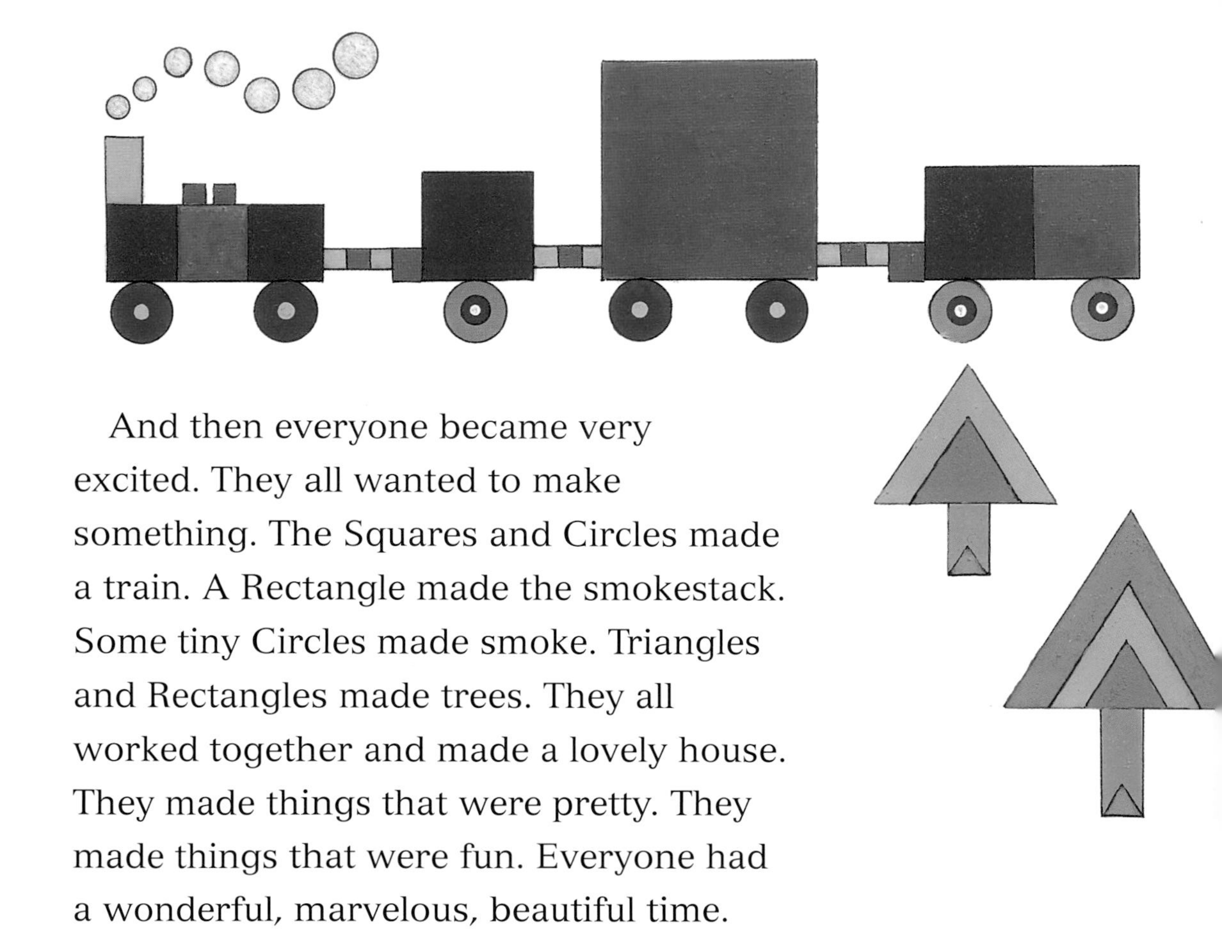

And then everyone became very excited. They all wanted to make something. The Squares and Circles made a train. A Rectangle made the smokestack. Some tiny Circles made smoke. Triangles and Rectangles made trees. They all worked together and made a lovely house. They made things that were pretty. They made things that were fun. Everyone had a wonderful, marvelous, beautiful time.

When it was time to go home, they all sang a little song: "We are glad! glad! glad! Being different is not bad!"

And they sang it over and over, all the way home.

The grown-ups in your life can help you learn right from wrong.

Learning Right from Wrong

How do you know what is right?

How do you know what is wrong?

These are not easy questions to answer. However, looking for the answers to such questions can help you know yourself and the world around you. You will not find all the answers right away, but you will find the beginnings of the answers. Your understanding will grow as you grow.

You were not born knowing right from wrong. You learn this as you grow. You learn by talking and listening to people you can trust. You learn by watching and copying what the people around you say and do.

As you learn right from wrong, you will make mistakes. It is okay to make mistakes. You can learn from mistakes. You can change how you do things because of your experiences.

A feeling inside you tells you when something seems right or wrong.

There is a feeling inside you that helps you decide what to do. Sometimes it is called an "inner voice" or "gut feeling." Sometimes it tells you when something feels right. Other times it might say "uh-oh." Then you know something may not be right. Your inner voice can help guide you in everything you do.

Losing a Loved One

Have you ever had a pet that died? It hurts. It does not hurt like when you fall and scrape your knee. It is a different kind of pain. It makes you feel sad.

The death of your pet means that you will never see it again. Sometimes people die, too—people you love. This means that you will never see them again in this world. It hurts a lot.

When someone's friend or relative dies, it is very painful. They miss that person. They feel lonely, strange, and sad. They may become quiet and want to be left alone. They want to think about the person who has

Looking at pictures is a good way to remember the happy times you shared with a loved one.

died. They may feel angry that the person has left them. The sadness or anger after someone has died is called grieving (GREEV ihng). People who grieve are trying to understand and accept the death of someone they love.

Grieving takes time. Many people feel they will always miss the person who has died. But after a while, people begin to remember their loved one with happiness. They remember good times they shared.

Pets and people never leave you completely. They live on in your memories. In this way, they are part of you forever.

The love you feel for a pet can be very strong.

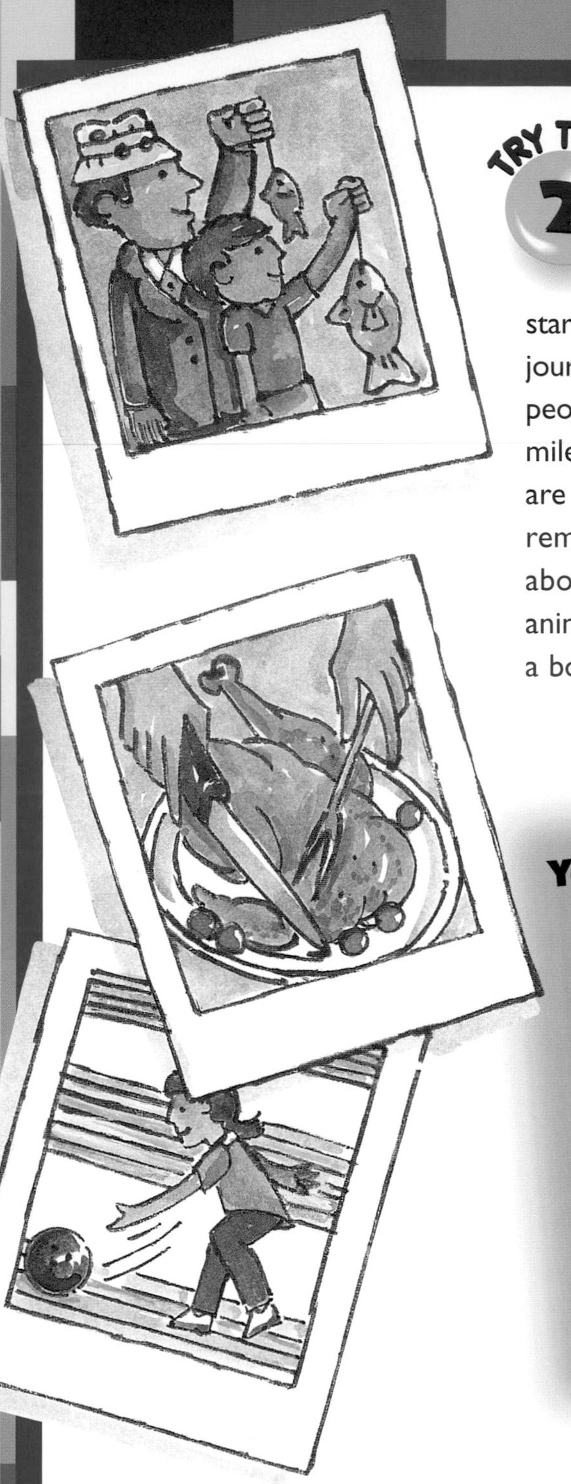

TRY THIS! 2 Make a Memory Book

Birthdays, vacations, and starting school are milestones on your journey through life. Losing pets and people who are close to you also are milestones. In between the milestones are other special times. A good way to remember your thoughts and feelings about special moments, people, and animals is to collect your memories in a book.

You Will Need:

- heavy paper
- a pencil or pen
- crayons or markers
- copies or scans of photographs
- mementos, such as programs, brochures, ticket stubs, or stickers
- glue
- a fine-line marker
- a three-hole punch
- yarn, brass fasteners, or a three-ring binder

What To Do:

1. Gather photographs and mementos of the special moments you would like to remember. Get permission to use them first, or make copies or scans. Or draw your own pictures.

2. Arrange your pictures and mementos on the heavy paper. Then glue them in place.

3. Use a fine-line marker or pen to write information about the pictures and objects. Include dates, places, and your feelings. Draw fancy borders, too. If you need help, ask an adult.

4. Make a cover for your book.

5. Put your pages in any order you like. Use the three-hole punch to make holes along one side of each page. Fasten the pages together using yarn or brass fasteners, or place them in a three-ring binder. If you use a binder, you can tape your cover to the front of the binder. Leave blank pages at the back so you can add more memories as you grow.

Share your book with friends and family.

Taking Care of Yourself

You take care of your toys, your books, and your bike. But the most important thing to take care of is your body.

There are many things you can do to make sure your body stays fit and healthy. You can exercise, eat the right kinds and amounts of food, and get plenty of sleep. The better you take care of yourself, the happier you will probably be.

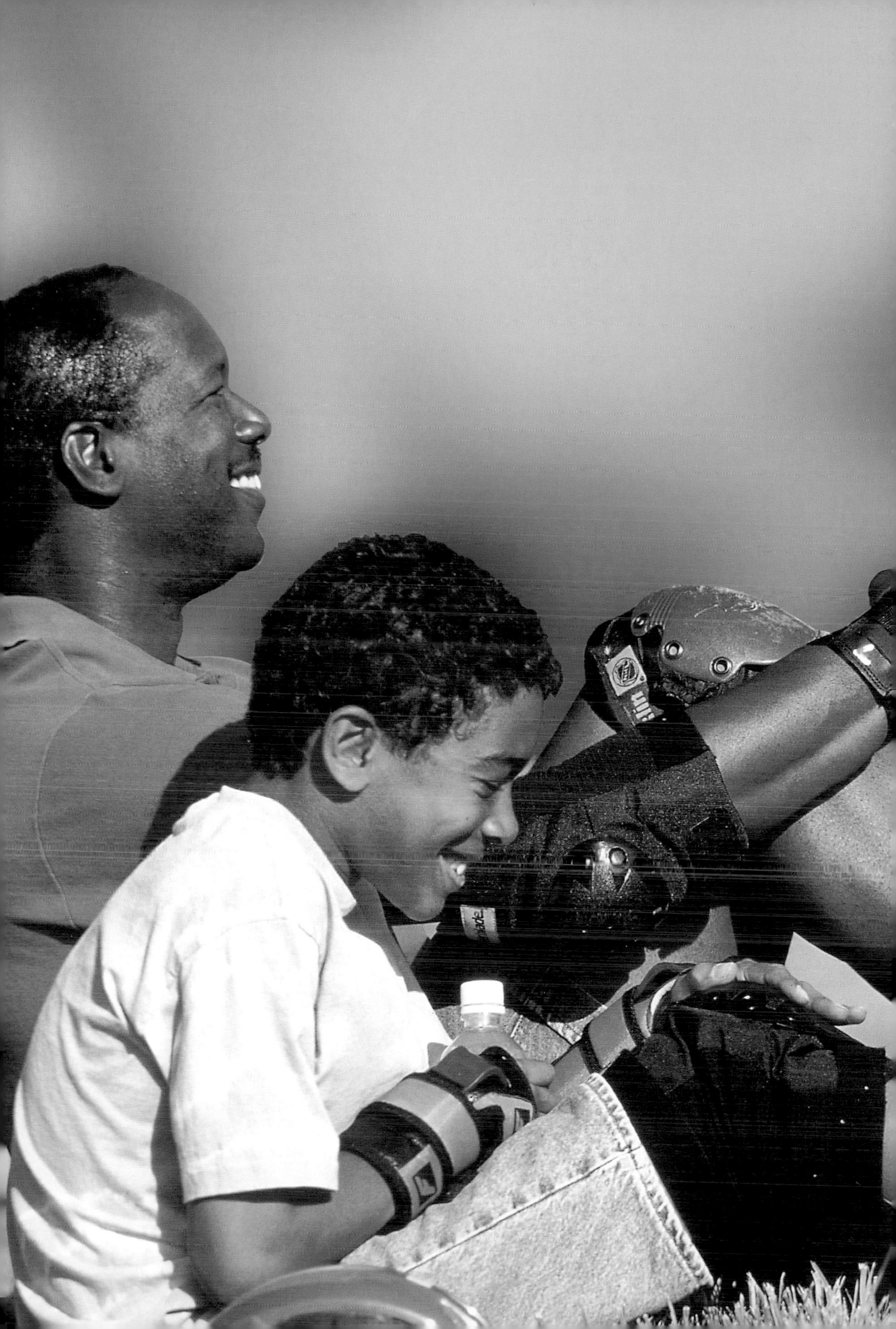

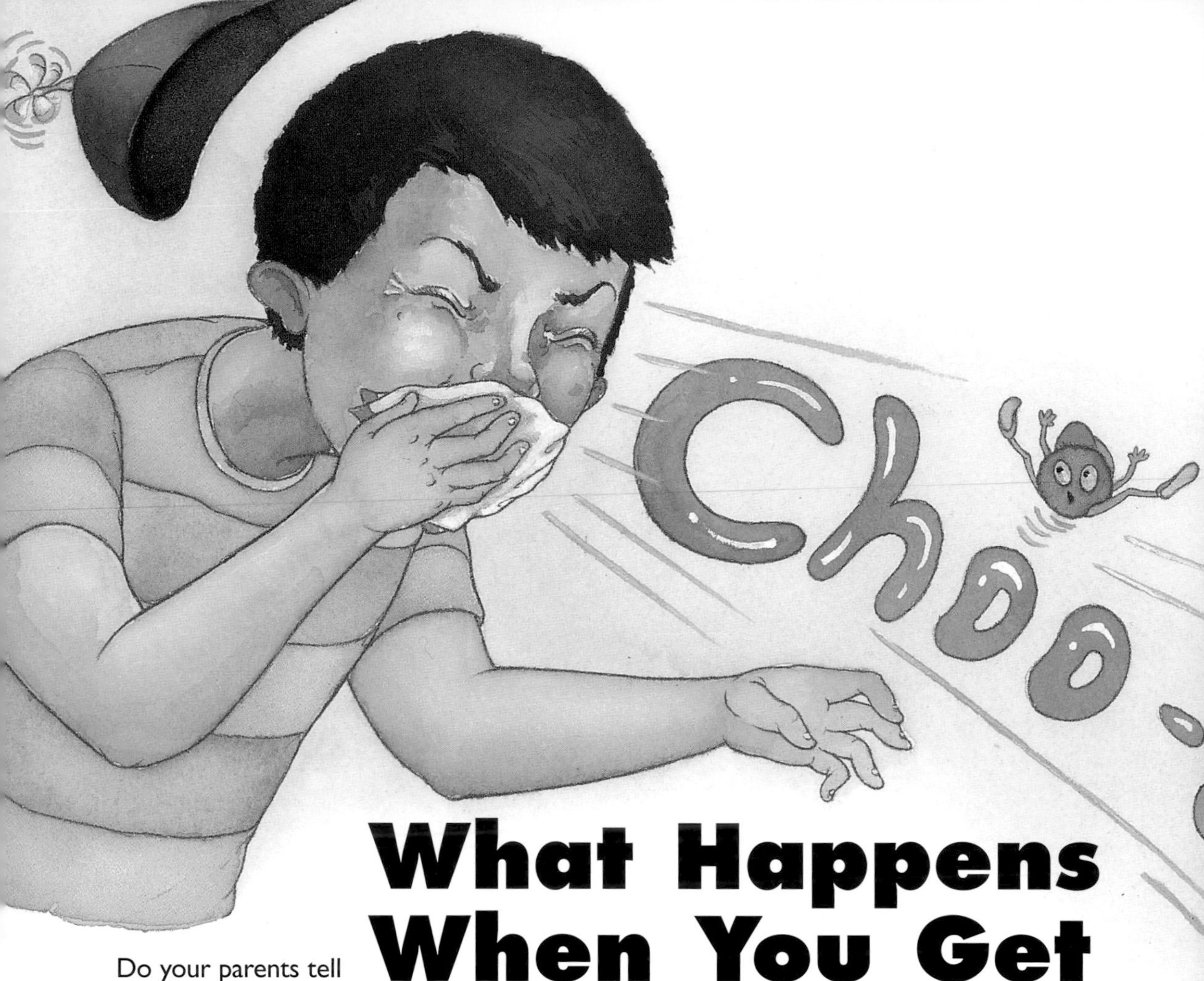

What Happens When You Get Sick?

Do your parents tell you to cover your nose and mouth when you sneeze? That's because when you sneeze, tiny drops of fluid spray out of your mouth. Tiny germs travel in that fluid and can make other people sick too.

Have you had chickenpox or measles, a cold, an ear infection, or the flu? If so, your body was under attack!

When you get sick, tiny germs called viruses (VY ruhs uhz) or bacteria (bak TEER ee uh) attack your body. Some of these germs travel from person to person in the drops of fluid that shoot out of the mouth during a sneeze or cough. Some are spread in food and water. These germs can make you feel sick.

Luckily your body fights back. And sometimes medicine helps your body fight the germs.

After you have been sick with certain illnesses, your body remembers the germs. If one of the germs tries to attack again, your body destroys it as soon as it enters your body. That's why you usually get some illnesses, like chickenpox, only once.

You can get some illnesses, like colds and the flu, over and over again. This is because there are so many kinds of cold and flu viruses. If a new virus invades your body, your body does not know that virus, and so you get sick.

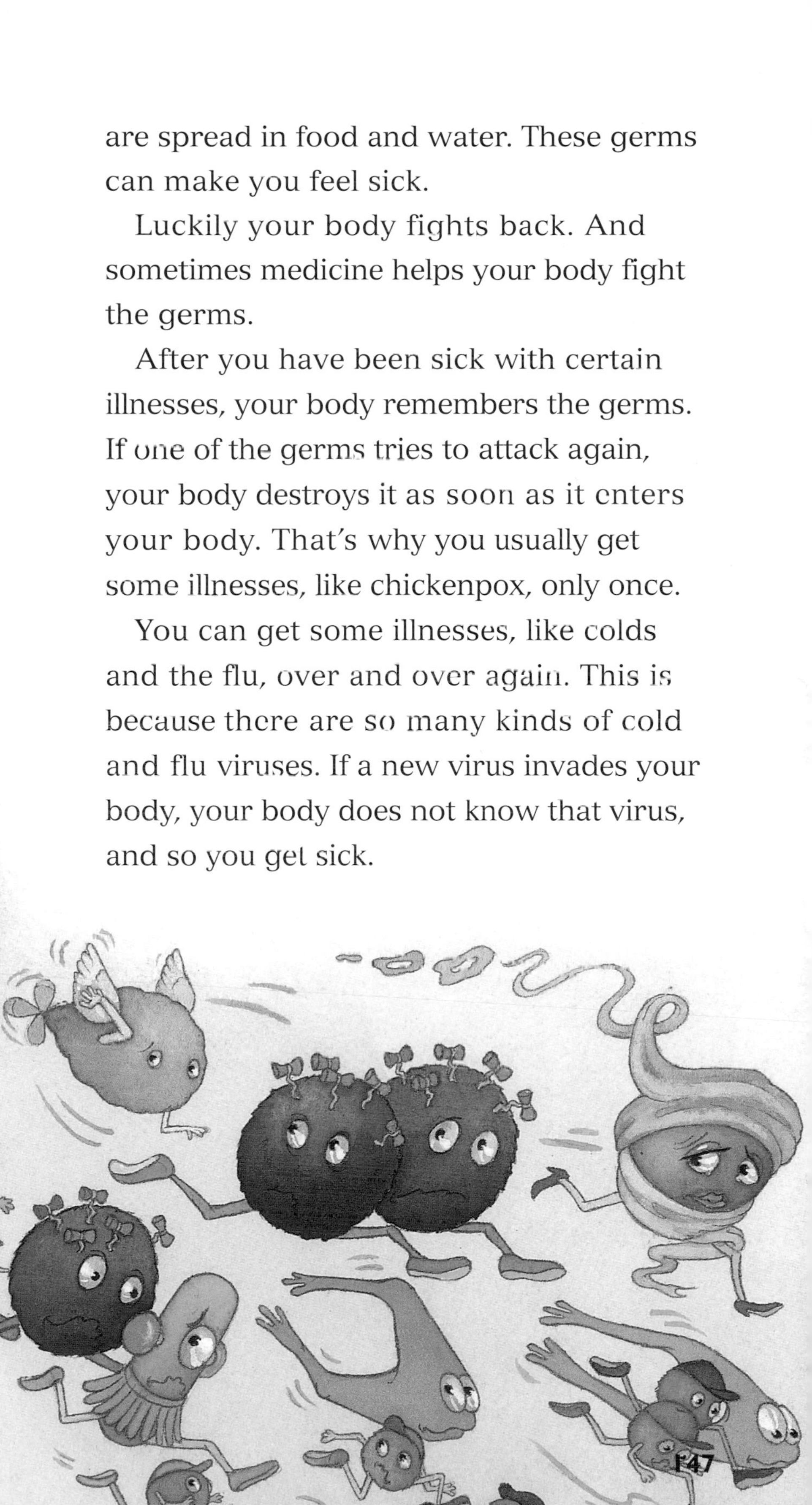

Your body knows how to heal a cut.

How Does Your Body Heal Itself?

You are rolling along on your bike when suddenly you hit a stone on the road. You fall and cut your hand. It is bleeding and it hurts.

Right away, your body begins fixing the cut. Your cells quickly jump into action and do their special jobs.

Cleaning and covering a cut quickly can help it to heal.

When you cut yourself, you begin to bleed. Almost at once the blood begins to clot. The cells stick together. Slowly, the blood gets thick and covers the cut. Then the blood dries and gets hard. It makes a kind of cover, called a scab, over the cut.

The cells along the edges of the cut grow and divide. New cells take the place of some of those that were hurt by the cut.

Still other cells do another kind of job. These are special healing cells. They make a kind of net that joins the edges of the cut together. Each day this net gets thicker, tougher, and stronger.

Soon the scab falls off. Then you can see the new skin underneath. Your body has healed itself.

KNOW It All!

Sometimes a deep cut leaves a mark on your skin, even after it has healed. That mark is called a scar. A scar forms when a deep layer of skin has been damaged. Scars may be red at first but the color usually fades over time.

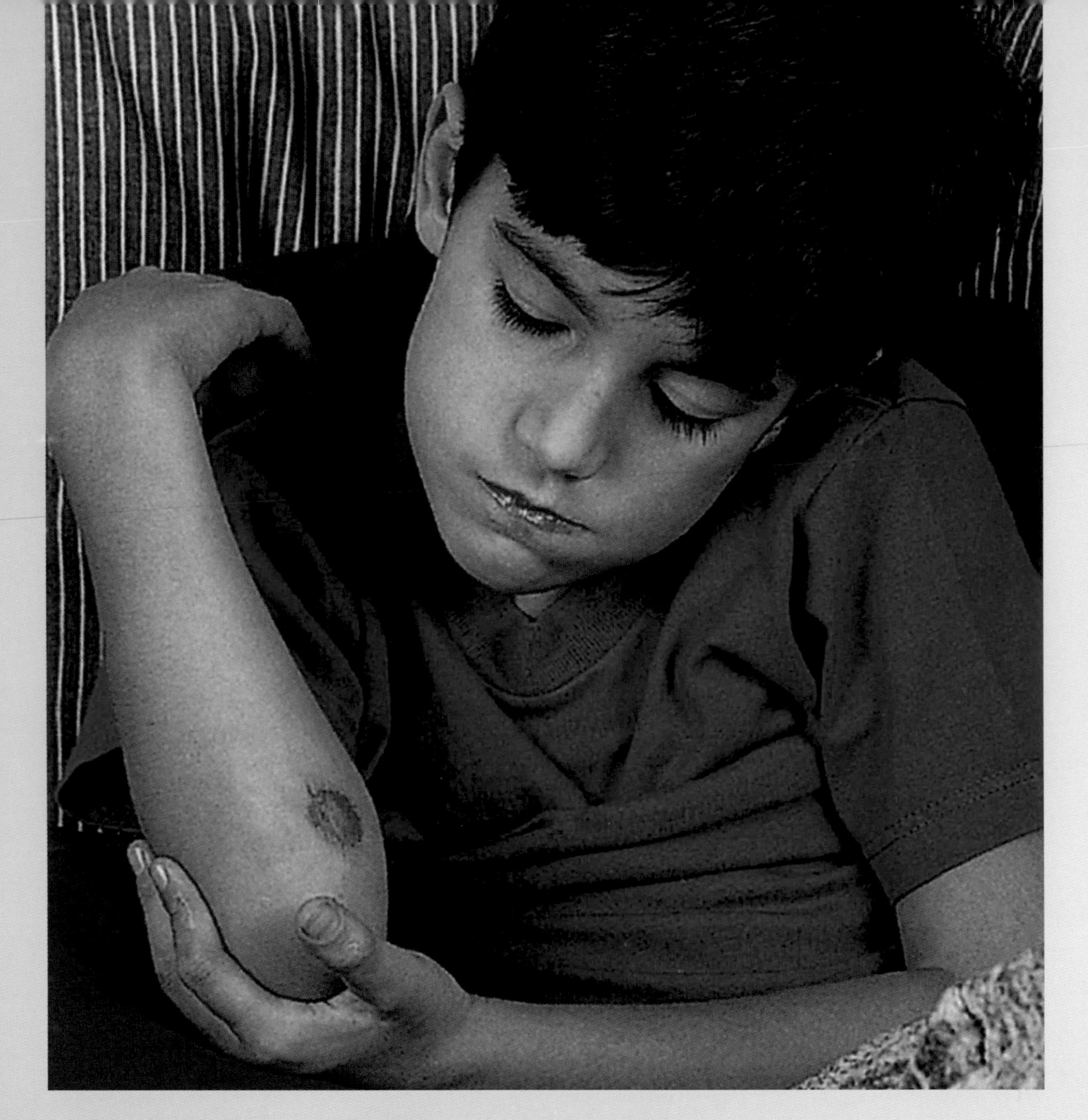

A bruise usually starts out blue or black. It changes colors as it heals.

Bumps, Bruises, and Blisters

Sometimes when you bump a part of your body, such as your elbow, the bump pushes a muscle against a bone. Tiny veins and arteries in the muscle break. Some blood leaks out, and soon, you have a bruise.

A bruise is kind of like an inside-out cut. A bruise does not bleed on the outside because the skin is not broken. Instead, the blood moves below the top layer of your skin. The blood shows through your skin as dark blue or black.

You can get a blister when your skin rubs against something over and over again. Your hands may get blisters from holding tightly to your bicycle handlebars. You might get a blister on your foot where it rubs against the shoe.

As the bruise heals, it may change color. Each color is lighter than the last. This means that the blood is moving back into your body. The muscle is getting well.

Burns are another way you can hurt yourself. When your skin burns, the burned spot puffs up. A blister forms. A blister is like a puffy little pocket in the layers of your skin. The top layer of skin pulls away from the layers underneath it, and the space fills with liquid. The top layer keeps germs from getting into the blister.

Again, your cells start to heal your burned skin. Slowly the liquid moves back into your body, and your blister heals.

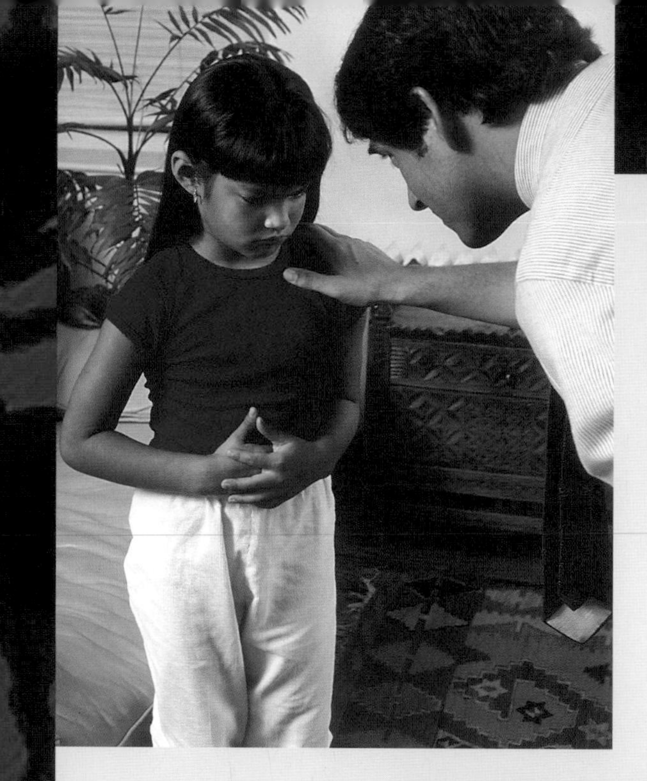

Everyone feels pain differently. An injury that causes a lot of pain in one person might cause only a little bit of pain in another person.

What Pain Tells You

Once in a while, some part of your body hurts. It may be your stomach or your head. You feel pain.

It is never fun to feel pain. Sometimes you might even cry. Pain is a warning. Pain usually happens because you are sick or have hurt part of your body. When you feel pain, nerves send a signal to your brain. Your brain understands the signal. If you did not feel pain, you would not know when something was wrong inside.

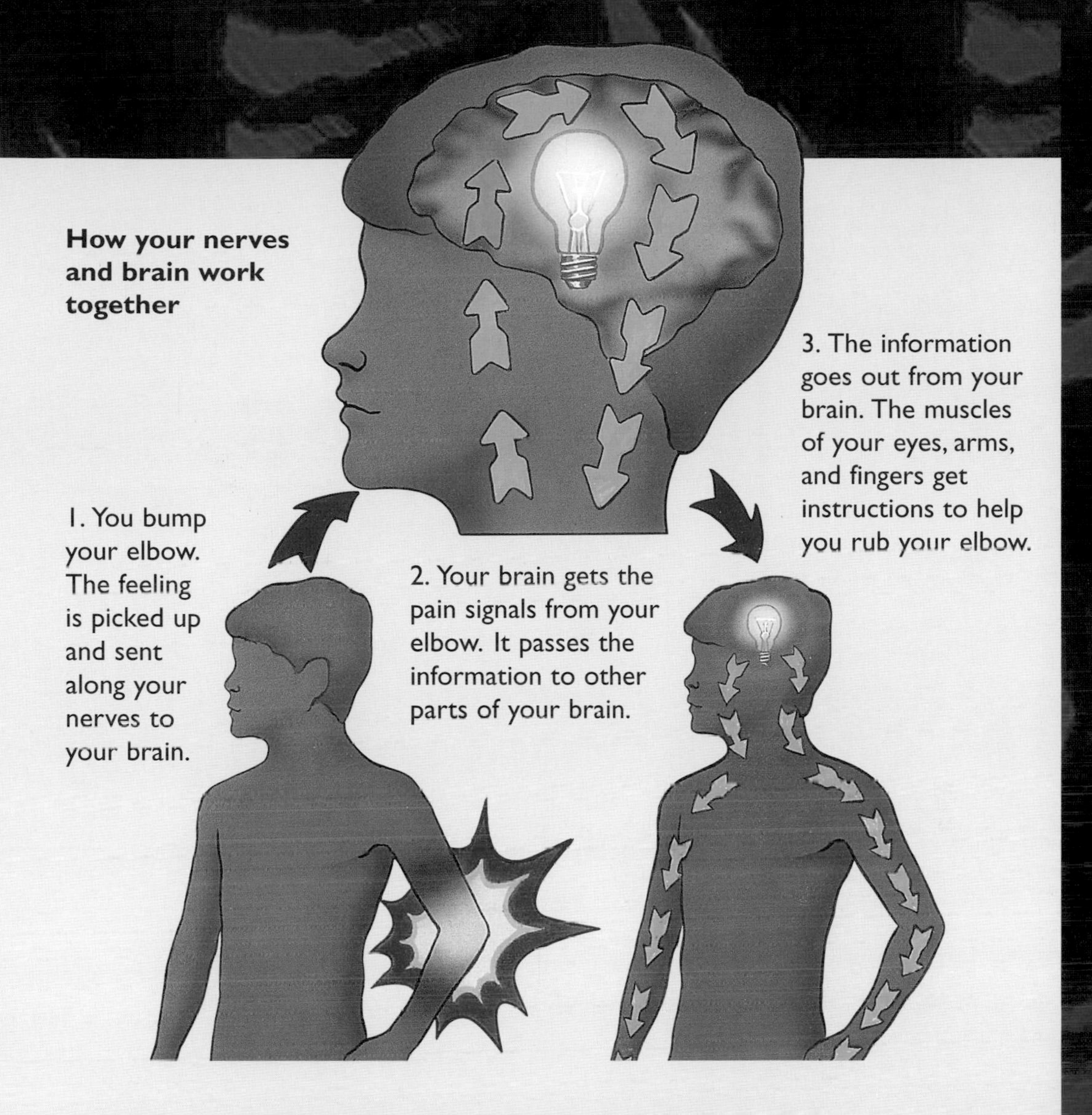

When you feel pain, tell your parents or your teacher where it hurts. They may know how to make the pain feel better. For example, if you have a headache, your mother might suggest sleep, an ice pack, or medicine to help take the pain away. Other times you may need to see your doctor. Your doctor might have to do medical tests to find out what is wrong and how to make you feel better.

This patient is being weighed and measured.

Visiting the Doctor

Sometimes you go to the doctor when you are sick. Other times you go when you are not sick at all. This kind of visit is called a checkup.

Checkups are a good way for you and your doctor to see how well you are growing. It is also a good time for you to ask questions about your body and your health.

The nurse usually begins your checkup by measuring your height and weight. The nurse and doctor keep track of how much you weigh and how tall you are at each visit. This is the best way for your doctor to see how well you are growing.

Next, the doctor listens through a **stethoscope** (STETH uh SKOHP) to different sounds inside your body. The earpieces of the stethoscope fit in the doctor's ears. The flat round part of the stethoscope is placed over the part of your body the doctor wants to hear.

The doctor holds the stethoscope on your chest and listens to the sound of your heart beating. The sound your

The doctor is letting this patient listen to her own heart.

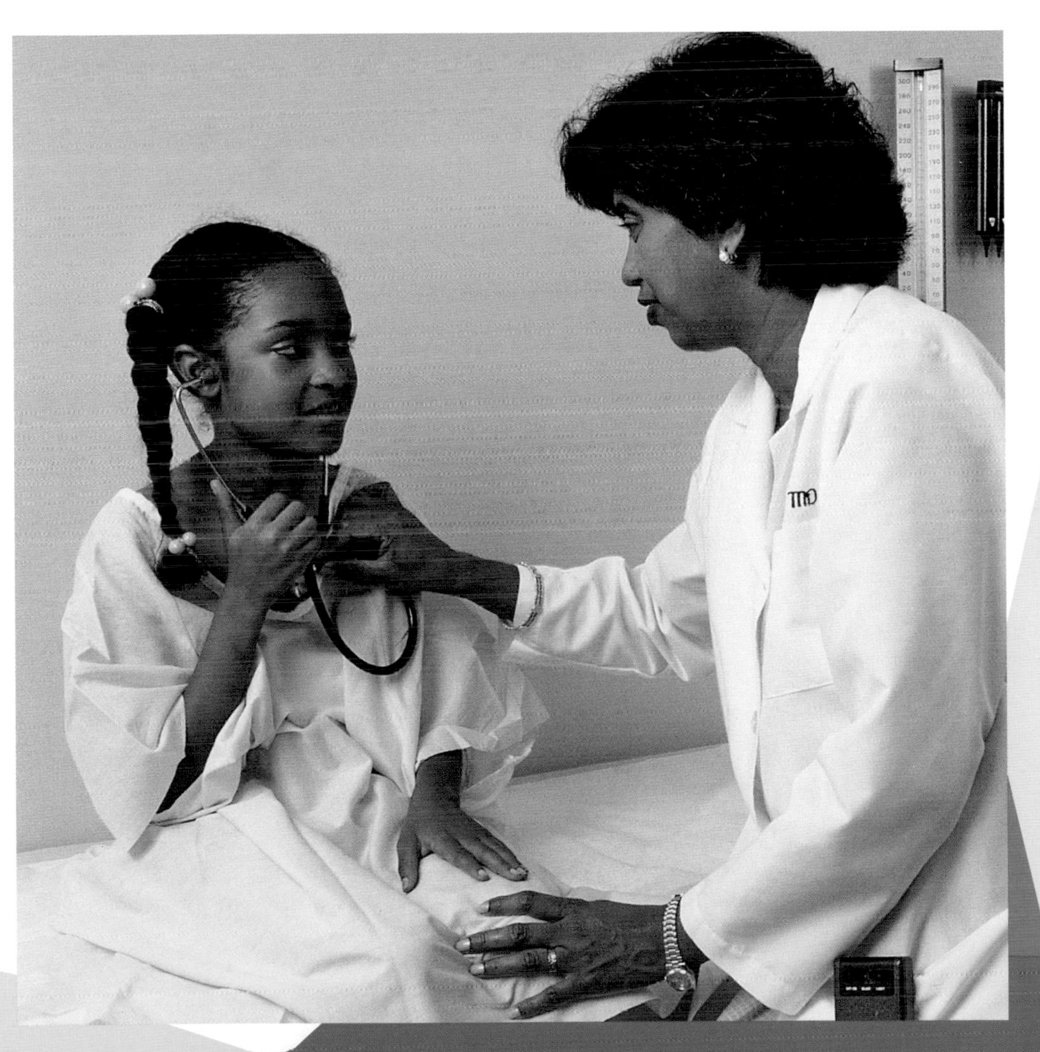

heart makes is something like this: *lub-dub, lub-dub, lub-dub.* Then the doctor moves the stethoscope around on your chest and back to hear your breathing. The doctor will ask you to take a few deep breaths. If you are healthy, your lungs do not make much noise.

Then the doctor shines a light into your eyes. The light helps the doctor look at the inside of your eyes. You might have to read some letters on a chart. The doctor wants to be sure you can see well.

The doctor or nurse might ask you about the foods you eat, how much you sleep, and if you exercise. These are all important questions. To stay healthy, you need to eat healthy foods and get enough rest and exercise. Your doctor may give you some ideas about how to do these things.

Next, the doctor shines a light into your ears. The doctor wants to be sure that all your ear openings are clear. If they are not, you may not be able to hear well.

KNOW It All!

At certain checkups, your doctor will give you one or more immunization (IHM yoo nih ZAY shuhn) shots. These shots help keep you healthy. Some shots hurt. But the little bit of pain you feel may save you a lot of sickness later. Some medicine has to be in shots, because your body would digest the medicine if you swallowed it, the same way it digests food. Then the medicine would not be able to work as well to keep you healthy.

Why Is It Important to Eat Well?

Like a car, your body needs fuel to keep it running. Your body's fuel is food.

Food contains the things your body needs for energy. These include proteins (PROH teenz), fats, and carbohydrates (KAHR boh HY drayts).

Proteins provide energy and help make muscles, skin and other organs, and blood. They also help your body to fix itself. You can get protein from animal foods such as meat, fish, and milk products. You also can get protein from certain beans and nuts.

Fats provide a lot of energy. Your body needs some fats, but not too many. You can get fats when you eat meat, butter, certain oils, and some plant foods such as nuts, olives, and avocados.

Carbohydrates are the body's main source of energy. Many foods contain carbohydrates, including potatoes, pasta, and grains.

Food also contains vitamins and minerals. There are many different vitamins, such as vitamins A, C, and D. They all help keep your body healthy. Many fruits and vegetables have vitamins. There also are many different minerals, including calcium (KAL see uhm) and iron. Calcium is good for your bones and teeth. Iron is good for your blood.

Water may be the most important thing you can give your body. The body needs water to do all its work.

Mix It Up

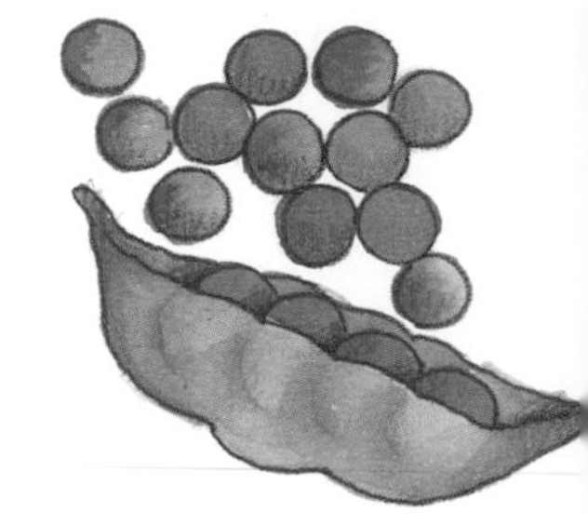

What are your favorite foods? Maybe you like fish, hamburgers, or scrambled eggs. These foods all can be part of a healthful diet. But they are not enough. That's because they are all proteins. Your body needs many different kinds of nutrients to stay healthy.

The best way to get all the nutrients your body needs is to eat many different kinds of food each day. When you eat a variety of foods, you can get the vitamins and minerals your body needs.

Eating a variety of foods means eating bread, rice, and other grains, especially whole grains. It means eating nuts and beans for protein. It also means eating meats, such as beef, fish, and chicken.

Dairy products, such as milk and cheese, are also important for a healthy diet. This food group is especially important for younger people, whose bones are still growing.

Finally, a wide variety of vegetables and fruit is very important for health. These foods contain vitamins and minerals that are critical to our well-being.

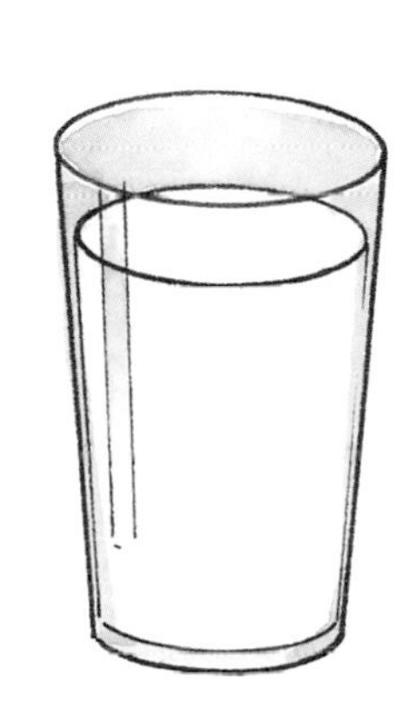

All foods that come in a package usually have food labels that tell you what is in the food. These labels can help you understand what food groups are contained in a given item. That helps you to look for items with more fruits or vegetables and fewer additives and preservatives.

Food labels also tell you how many fats, carbohydrates, and other nutrients are in one serving of that food. This helps you to choose foods that are lower in fats and sugar and higher in nutritional value.

A Guide to Food

The amount of energy food contains is measured in units called **calories.** How many calories you need to eat each day depends on a number of things—including how old you are and how active you are. The diet shown at right, for instance, would be good for an 11-year-old boy who is physically active for 30 to 60 minutes per day. No matter what your calorie needs are, a diet high in fruits, vegetables, grains, and dairy, but low in sugar and fats, will keep you feeling your best.

For a 2,000-calorie diet, you need the amounts shown below from each group.

Eat 2 cups of fruit per day. Eat a variety of fresh, frozen, canned, or dried fruit.

Eat 2 ½ cups of vegetables per day. Eat lots of dark-green, leafy vegetables, orange vegetables, and dry beans and peas.

Eat 6 ounces of grain foods—including at least 3 ounces of whole-grain foods—per day.

TRY THIS! 1

Keep a list of the kinds and amount of foods you eat in one day. Compare how many servings you ate from each food group with the number of servings suggested in the food pyramid on the Website http://www.mypyramid.gov. What food groups do most of your foods come from? Which group of foods do you need to eat more of? Share your results with a parent or doctor.

Get 3 cups of milk, yogurt, and other milk products per day. Choose milk products that are low-fat or fat-free.

Eat 5 ½ ounces of meat and beans per day. Choose low-fat or lean meats and poultry. Vary your protein routine by choosing fish, beans, peas, nuts, and seeds.

Limit fats, sugars, and salt (sodium). Make most of your fat sources fish, nuts, and vegetable oils.

Make a Breakfast Sundae

Ready to try something new and good for you? Enjoy this tasty, healthful treat any day of the week!

You Will Need:

- 3 kinds of fresh fruit, such as sliced strawberries, blueberries, sliced peaches, sliced bananas, grapes, or sliced apples
- a bowl
- 1 small container low-fat or non-fat yogurt, any flavor
- a spoon
- granola
- raisins

What To Do:

1. Wash your hands.
2. Rinse the fruits and put them into the bowl. If you need to slice the fruit, ask an adult for help.
3. Spoon the yogurt on top of the fruit.
4. Sprinkle on a little granola.
5. Sprinkle on some raisins.

Eat. Yum!

Snack Kabobs

These healthful snacks are fun to make and eat with a friend!

You Will Need:

thick slices or chunks of fruits such as pineapple, pear, and banana
cubes of cheese
chunks of cooked meat, such as chicken and ham
raw vegetables, such as cucumbers, zucchini, lettuce and whole cherry tomatoes
toothpicks or pretzel sticks

What To Do:

1. Wash your hands.
2. Clean the fruits and vegetables. Then ask an adult to help you slice the fruits, cheeses, meat, and vegetables.
3. On a toothpick or pretzel stick, put a combination of any of the foods listed here.

Which combination makes your mouth water?

English Muffin Pizza

This recipe shows how to make enough pizza for you and a friend!

You Will Need:

1 English muffin, sliced in two halves
1/2 cup (113 grams) tomato sauce
pizza toppings, such as green peppers, mushrooms, onions
1/4 cup (56 grams) mozzarella cheese, shredded

What To Do:

1. Ask an adult to help you preheat the oven or toaster oven to 400 °F (204 °C).
2. Wash your hands.
3. Place the muffin halves on a cookie sheet. Spread tomato sauce on top of the muffins.
4. Layer your favorite toppings on top of the sauce.
5. Sprinkle cheese over the toppings.
6. Ask an adult to help you bake the pizza for five minutes, or until the cheese melts. Enjoy!

What Is Junk Food?

You wake up one morning. Your mother asks, "What would you like for breakfast—potato chips, cheese curls, ice cream, candy, or soda pop?"

You think to yourself, "Am I dreaming?"

Yes, you are.

TRY THIS! 1

How well can you tell junk foods from healthful foods? Which of the following foods would you say are junk foods?

- potato chips
- whole-wheat bread
- raisins
- french fries
- chocolate candy
- sprinkle cookies
- baked potato
- soda pop
- yogurt
- jelly beans

See answers on next page.

Your parents try to limit how much junk food you eat for a reason. Too much junk food is not good for your body.

Junk foods are called "junk" because they contain a lot of substances your body does not need. Some contain a lot of sugar. Others have a lot of fat—far more than your body needs.

But many people eat a whole lot of junk food. And if all you ate was junk food, you would soon be very unhealthy. You would not get enough of the things your body needs, such as protein, vitamins, and fiber. And you would have too much of the things you need only a little of, such as sugar, salt, and fat.

It would not hurt your body if you never ate any junk foods. They are fun to eat, though. Happily, a little junk food now and then will not hurt you.

Are french fries junk food?

Answers: potato chips, french fries, chocolate candy, sprinkle cookies, soda pop, and jelly beans are junk foods.

Exercising Your Body

Go ahead—run, jump, skip, climb! Not only is it fun, it's good for you, too. Your body parts need exercise to stay healthy.

There are different kinds of exercise. Some build your muscles. Some strengthen your heart and lungs. A strong heart and lungs are better at getting oxygen to the rest of your body. Exercises that build your muscles include climbing ropes and monkey bars. You can also try handstand contests, walking on your hands, walking

on all fours, and doing pushups while on your knees.

Walking, running, swimming, playing soccer, dancing, and cycling are all aerobic (air OH bihk) exercises. They help make your heart and lungs strong. What is your favorite aerobic exercise? Try it for at least 20 minutes, and you can feel your heart beat faster.

Shape up and you'll be ready for anything—a sports game, a busy day, and a healthy life.

TRY THIS! 1

Before you exercise, warm up your body. Warm muscles stretch more easily and are less likely to get hurt. Walk, slowly skip rope, or gently jog in place. These activities increase the blood flow to your muscles. Do these again at the end of exercising. This lets your body cool down slowly.

Nonsugary snacks, such as fruits and vegetables, help keep your teeth healthy.

Looking After Your Teeth

There is a war going on inside your mouth! The enemy is **plaque** (plak), a sticky white coating that grows on teeth. Plaque destroys the outsides of teeth by sending out an army of acids. It sends poisons into the gums.

How can you fight back? The handiest weapon you have is your toothbrush. Brush with small, round movements to clean the outside of your teeth. Then move the toothbrush up and down to clear away the plaque between your teeth. To hold back plaque, your dentist may also tell you to floss your teeth at least once a day.

You also can help your teeth by choosing healthful foods. The more often you eat sugary things, the worse it is for your teeth. As soon as something sugary is around, plaque sends out a new army of acids. The more often you eat sweets, the more acid you have to fight. That's why dentists suggest that you eat snacks such as fruits and vegetables.

If you do eat sugary things, eat them at mealtimes and brush your teeth soon afterward. Try to avoid sweet foods that stick to your teeth, such as sugary cereals and suckers.

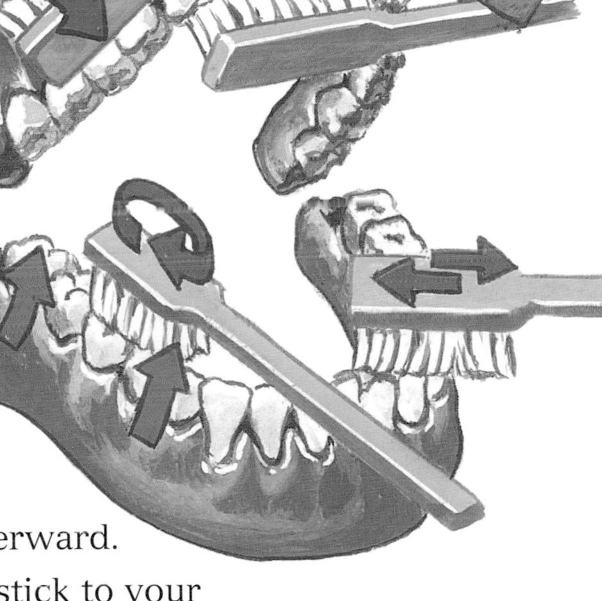

Use small, round movements and brush every tooth.

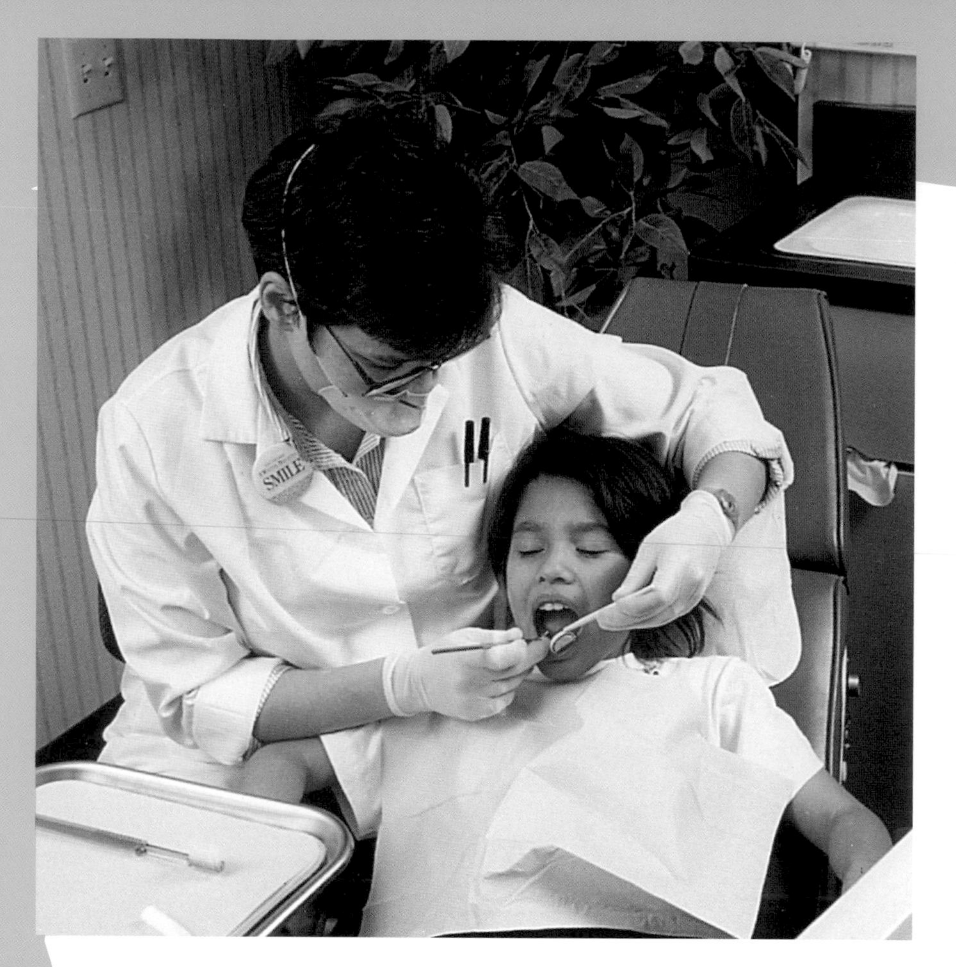

Your dentist uses special tools to check and clean your teeth.

Visiting the Dentist

Brushing your teeth several times a day and eating healthful foods are two ways to keep your teeth healthy and white. Another thing you can do is visit your dentist at least once a year.

At the dentist's office, you sit in a special chair. It moves so the dentist can look into your mouth easily. First, the dentist puts a little round mirror on a handle into your mouth. This helps the dentist see the sides of your teeth. To feel for cavities (KAV uh teez), or holes, in your teeth, the dentist uses tiny tools called explorers.

Your dentist or the hygienist (HY jeen ihst) then cleans and polishes your teeth to make them shine.

If your dentist finds a cavity in one of your teeth, it will need to be cleaned and filled. Before filling your tooth, your dentist may give you a shot in the gum near the tooth that has the cavity. The shot makes the area numb, so you cannot feel anything while the dentist works on your tooth.

Remember, the teeth you begin to get when you are only 6 years old have to last you the rest of your life. Take good care of them. Ask your dentist for a new toothbrush, toothpaste, and dental floss after each checkup.

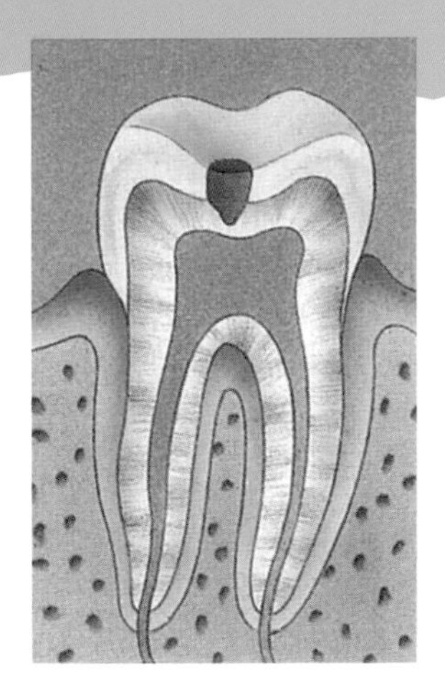

This tooth has a cavity. A cavity is a hole caused by bacteria. Even the gums are sick. You know this because they are red and puffy.

Here is a healthy tooth and gums. The tooth is white and the gums are pink.

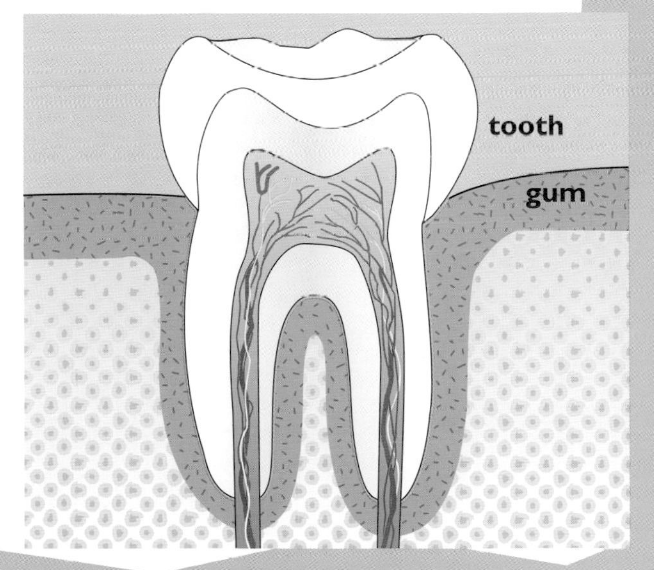

Why Do You Need Sleep?

Think about how you feel when you don't get enough sleep. You feel tired, you can't think very well, and you may get angry easily.

Sleep helps keep you healthy. When you sleep, your muscles rest. So does your brain.

People who get enough sleep each night are able to think more clearly. They do

Did you know that you move around in your bed about 12 times a night?

not make as many mistakes as people who do not get a good night's sleep. And they may react more quickly.

People who get enough sleep night after night also are better able to fight off diseases. They do not get as many colds and other illnesses as people who are always tired.

The best way to get a good night's sleep is to go to bed at the same time each night and wake up at the same time each morning. While you may want to sleep late on weekends, try not to. Oversleeping can keep you awake the next night.

The next time it's bedtime, give your brain a treat. Go to bed on time, and give it the rest it deserves.

TRY THIS! 1

If you have trouble falling asleep—or simply do not want to go to bed—try these ideas to make bedtime a good time:

- Listen to a book on tape or soft music.
- Imagine yourself in your favorite place.
- Think about what you did today, and what you will do tomorrow.
- Imagine sheep jumping over a fence one by one. Count each sheep as it jumps.

The Clean Scene

You have them on your fingers.
You have them in your hair.
Germs are all around you.
You'll find them everywhere.

You might think that looking clean is just something that adults worry about. But you should think about it too. Keeping yourself clean helps you stay free of harmful germs.

Whether you play, work, shop, or visit a friend, your hands pick up germs all day. If the germs get into your food, or if you lick your fingers or bite your nails, it is easy to see how the germs can get inside your body. But you do not have to let this happen.

You can get rid of the germs you collect. After going to the bathroom, wash your hands with soap and water—and don't forget the backs of your hands. Wash your hands before meals so germs don't get into your food—and inside you. Also wash your hands after sneezing and coughing, especially if you are sick.

The skin on other parts of your body picks up germs too. These germs may even cause an unpleasant odor. That is because they feed on the oil in sweat. Then they multiply and die—that's where the bad smell comes from. So take a bath or wash the places where you sweat most.

Keeping clean not only makes you feel good, it also helps you stay healthy.

TRY THIS! 1

Safety at Home

Being safe means staying away from danger or harm. Look at this picture of a home. It shows a child living safely at home. Try to match each numbered safety tip below to the part of the home it describes.

1. A rubber mat in the tub and a rubber-backed rug on the floor will help keep you from slipping on a wet surface.

2. To reach high shelves, always use a stepladder. Never use a chair or climb a bookshelf.

3. Always put away your shoes and toys so that no one trips over them.

4. Whenever you carry something that has a point, such as scissors or a sharpened pencil, walk with the point down.

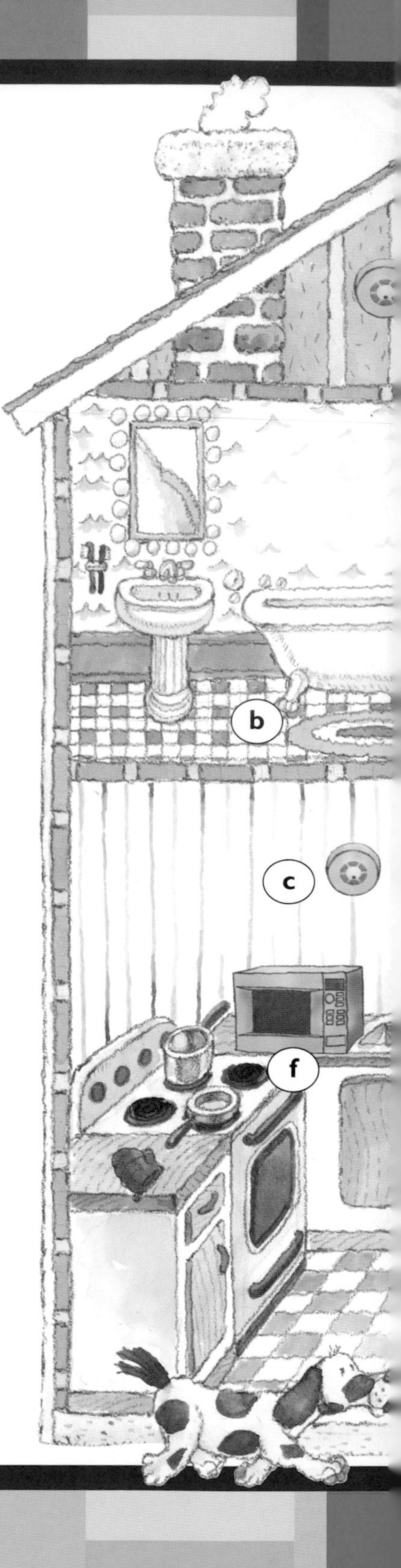

5. Ask an adult to show you the safe way to use toasters, microwave ovens, and other appliances. Never use these appliances without an adult's permission.

6. Never play with fire. If you find matches, give them to an adult.

7. Remind an adult in your home to change the batteries in your home's smoke alarms twice a year.

Answers: 1b; 2a; 3d; 4e; 5f; 6g; 7c.

Safety away from Home

Safety is not something you should leave at home. Take it with you everywhere you go. The picture on this page shows many things people are doing to keep safe. Can you find these safe actions in the picture?

a. Whenever you ride in a car, wear your seatbelt.

b. If you are walking, always keep your eyes and ears open. Watch and listen for cars, bicycles, skaters,

and other hazards around you. Cross roads only at crosswalks. Cross the street with a crossing guard or when the stoplight is green.

c. Whenever you ride a bicycle, inline skates, or a skateboard, wear a helmet. Make sure it fits properly. Wear wrist guards and knee pads to help protect you, too. Whenever you venture out on your wheels, make sure you obey all traffic rules.

d. At the park or playground, stay out of the way of people on swings or coming down slides. Do not stand on things that are not firm, such as seesaws and swings.

e. Never talk to strangers unless you are with an adult.

Now that you know some safety rules to follow away from home, look again at the picture. Can you find all the ways in which people are not playing it safe in the picture? *See answers below.*

Answers: child skating in street and without safety gear; child running in front of swing; two children crossing the street without the crossing guard and not looking for cars; child standing on seesaw; child walking dog it can't control.

Glossary

Here are some of the words you read in this book. Many of them may be new to you. Some are hard to pronounce. But since you will see them again, they are good words to know. Next to each word, you will see how to say it correctly: **pituitary** (pih TOO uh TAIR ee). The part shown in small capital letters is said a little more loudly than the rest of the word. The part in large capital letters is said the loudest. Under each word are one or two sentences that tell what the word means.

A

artery (AHR tuhr ee)
A tube that carries fresh blood away from the heart is an artery.

B

bile (byl)
A liquid stored in the gall bladder is called bile.

bladder (BLAD uhr)
The bladder is a stretchy, baglike organ that stores urine until the body is ready to get rid of it.

D

diaphragm (DY uh fram)
The large muscle that lies below your lungs is your diaphragm. It helps you breathe.

E

esophagus (ee SAHF uh guhs)
The long tube that connects your mouth and stomach is called the esophagus.

F

follicle (FAH luh kuhl)
A small pocket that hair grows from is a follicle.

G

gene (jeen)
A gene carries instructions for a particular trait, such as eye color or height. Many genes were passed along to you from both of your parents in the egg cell and sperm cell that joined to become you.

H

hormone (HAWR mohn)
A hormone is a substance that travels throughout the blood to control functions such as growth elsewhere in your body.

J

joints (joynts)
The places where bones come together are called joints. The joints allow your body to move or bend.

K

keratin (KEHR uh tihn)
Keratin is the main substance in hair and nails. It forms when certain kinds of cells die.

kidney (KIHD nee)
One of the two large organs behind your stomach is a kidney. Your two kidneys clean waste from your blood.

L

larynx (LAIR ingks)
The boxed-shaped structure at the top of your trachea is your larynx. It helps you speak and is sometimes called the voice box.

lungs (lungz)
The two spongy, stretchy bags used for breathing are your lungs. These organs are in your chest. They bring oxygen to your blood and take wastes out.

M

marrow (MAIR oh)
The soft, jellylike substance inside your bones is called marrow. Red marrow helps the body make blood.

melanin (MEHL uh nihn)
The substance in the body that makes skin dark is melanin. Freckles are clumps of melanin.

N

nutrients (NOO tree uhnts)
Nutrients are nourishing substances your body needs to grow and be healthy. You get nutrients by eating healthful foods.

O

ovary (OH vuh ree)
An ovary is one of two organs in girls that makes and stores egg cells.

oxygen (AHK suh juhn)
Oxygen is a gas found in the air. Animals and plants need oxygen to live.

P

penis (PEE nihs)
The part on a boy where urine leaves the body is the penis.

pituitary gland (pih TOO uh TAIR ee gland)
The pituitary gland is a small gland located in the brain. It produces hormones that make your body grow. It also controls many other glands.

plaque (plak)
A sticky substance that forms when bits of food and bacteria stick to your teeth is called plaque. Plaque causes cavities. Brushing and flossing help get rid of plaque.

pore (pohr)
One of many tiny holes in the skin is a pore. Sweat comes out of your pores.

S

saliva (suh LY vuh)
Saliva is the liquid released in your mouth. It helps break down food to make it easier to swallow.

scrotum (SKROH tuhm)
The part of a boy's body that contains the testicles is the scrotum.

skeleton (SKEHL uh tuhn)
All your bones connected together make up your skeleton. Your skeleton gives shape to your body.

stethoscope (STEHTH uh skohp)
An instrument that a doctor uses to listen to sounds inside your body is a stethoscope.

T

tendon (TEHN duhn)
A tendon is a strong band or cord of tissue. It joins a muscle to a bone or to some other body part.

testicle (TEHS tuh kuhl)
A testicle is one of two glands in a boy's scrotum. When a boy grows up, the testicles make sperm cells.

tissue (TIHSH oo)
A group of similar cells working together, such as muscle cells in muscle tissue.

trachea (TRAY kee uh)
The tube through which air travels from your nose and mouth to your lungs is your trachea. It is also called the windpipe.

U

umbilical cord (uhm BIHL uh kuhl kawrd)
The umbilical cord is the cord that joins a baby to its mother before birth. A baby receives food and oxygen through this cord. After a baby is born, the cord is cut. The scar that is left is called the navel.

unique (yoo NEEK)
To be unique is to be one of a kind.

urethra (yoo REE thruh)
The tube that leads from your bladder out of your body is your urethra. It carries liquid waste products your body cannot use.

urine (YOOR uhn)
The liquid waste product made by your kidneys is called urine.

uterus (YOO tuhr uhs)
The uterus is an organ in a girl's body. When a girl grows up, the uterus can hold and nourish a developing baby.

V

vagina (vuh JY nuh)
The part of a girl's body that leads from the uterus out of the body is the vagina.

vein (vayn)
One of many tubes in your body that carry blood back to your heart is a vein.

Index

This index is an alphabetical list of important topics covered in this book. It will help you find information given in both words and pictures. To help you understand what an entry means, there is sometimes a helping word in parentheses, for example, **back** (part of body). If there is information in both words and pictures, you will see the words *with pictures* in parentheses after the page number. If there is only a picture, you will see the word *picture* in parentheses after the page number.